THE POWER OF PASSION

BRIAN M. GAZZARD

WESTBOW·
PRESS
A DIVISION OF THOMAS NELSON
& ZONDERVAN

Cover by Zigmars Batarevskis

Scripture taken from the New King James Version®. Copyright© 1982
Used by permission. Verses noted TLB are from The Living Bible ©1971
by Tyndale House Foundation, Wheaton, Illinois US 60189.

WestBow Press books may be ordered through booksellers or by contacting:

WestBow Press
A Division of Thomas Nelson & Zondervan
1663 Liberty Drive
Bloomington, IN 47403
www.westbowpress.com
1 (866) 928-1240

ISBN: 978-1-4908-6808-0 (sc)
ISBN: 978-1-4908-6809-7 (hc)
ISBN: 978-1-4908-6807-3 (e)

Library of Congress Control Number: 2015901286

Printed in the United States of America.

WestBow Press rev. date: 4/28/2015

This book is dedicated to

the partners of

HIGHER THAN AN EAGLE

and

especially to

June

who truly believed!

PREFACE

Effective communication is always a challenge.
It depends not only on a knowledge of the subject
but an understanding of the audience to whom
the communication is directed.
The audience for this book is obviously
not the academic community
for it is not a work of theology to be discussed.
Rather, the audience consists of men and
women who are tested daily
with issues that threaten to diminish their peace of mind
and ability to succeed in achieving their goals.
It is therefore a book with the object of
enabling people to meditate on
certain aspects of a transforming faith and thereby enrich their lives
through the development of a relevant, passionate faith.

I have always been impressed by the Gospel
writer's description of Jesus'
communication style:
"The common people heard Him gladly…"[1]

**"…for He taught them as one having
authority and not as the scribes."**[2]

This book seeks to follow that style of 'truth through illustration'
in the hope and expectation that that
spiritual truth will have a more
immediate and transformative impact in
the mind and heart of the reader.

My acknowledgements for certain materials are noted,
though after many years of listening to sermons
and researching preaching material,
many original sources are hard to identify.
So with the Apostle Paul I can say:
"I am a debtor both to...[3]

"the Jew first and also...the Greek."[4]

This book is especially dedicated to the partners and viewers of the
'Higher Than An Eagle' television program.
They have faithfully supported this ministry with their substance
as well as their prayers.
I am deeply grateful to Carol Hegadorn and
June Purvis for their extensive
work in helping to complete this work.

So, enjoy your meditation on "passion"
and may you become empowered to fully
live your purpose on earth.

••••••••••••••••••••••••••••

"WHERE IS THE LOVE?"

Suicide is both tragic and terrible.
Loss of an individual's potential is always tragic,
but such tragedy is made terrible when
exposed to the power of the internet.

The fact that we live in an increasingly dysfunctional world
was dramatically illustrated by this incident from Florida.
Modern technology takes both our
knowledge, and our dysfunction,
to ever heightened, and often negative, extremes!

A network news reporter told of a Florida teenager,
who used a webcam to live stream his suicide.
He was encouraged by the other people on his website.
"People were egging him on and saying things
like, 'go ahead and do it, faggot',"
said an investigator at the Broward County
Medical Examiner's office.

Abraham Biggs, 19, had been blogging on an
online body-building message board
and had linked his page to Justin.tv, a
live video streaming Web site,
where the camera rolled as he overdosed on prescription pills.

The teenager, who had been discussing his suicide on the forums,
also posted a suicide note on a body-building forum.
In the note he wrote, "I hate myself and I hate living."

"I have let everyone down and I feel as though
I will never change or improve.
I am in love with a girl and I know that
I am not good enough for her.
I have come to believe that my life has all been meaningless.
I keep trying and I keep failing.
I have thought about and attempted suicide many times in the past."

And so this 19-year-old died amidst the
varied blogged comments of viewers,
ranging from "OMG" - internet slang for "oh my god",
and "LOL", an abbreviation for "laughing out loud".

A social media strategist said that while public deaths are not new,
online chat rooms provide an especially accessible
forum for those debating suicide.
"The social Web tends to create a sideshow
atmosphere, like public executions in the 1700s.
The anonymity and lack of personal connection
bring out the worst in people."

And so this teen died to the accompaniment
of encouraging expletives.
Abraham Biggs was pronounced dead at 3:30 p.m., November 19th,
about 12 hours after he had begun blogging about his suicide.

The Internet has become THE new place for venting
pain (or inflicting pain), loneliness, and desperation,
with a resultant chorus of apathy, indifference or even
encouragement for "negative acts" by viewers.
Bullying via the net seems to be the 'avant
garde' practice of the young.

As I recount this tragedy, there's the haunting
refrain in my mind of the Roberta Flack and
Donny Hathaway's 1972 song "**Where is the Love?**"
It was a totally different age
with the relative naiveté of the previous
generation reflected in that song,
perhaps gone for good!

"Where is the love?" you ask.
Simply update the lyrics to the song produced
by the Black Eyed Peas in 2003[1]
and you see the "strange" new world:

WHERE IS THE LOVE?

**What's wrong with the world mama
People livin' like they ain't got no mamas
I think the whole world addicted to drama
Only attracted to things that'll bring you trauma**

What a difference a generation and "www" (world wide web) make!
Welcome to our "strange" new world!

There is a classic story of a grandfather and his grandson
walking through a forest one winter evening.
From far away they heard wolves howling.
"Hungry wolves!" said the grandson.
"Yes, just like the ones inside us," said the grandfather.
"What do you mean?" asked the boy.
"Do we have wolves inside us - hungry wolves?"
"Yes, we do. Two wolves."
"Two wolves?"
The grandfather stated, "One wolf is always angry and resentful.
Greedy. Full of false pride. Self-pity and arrogance.
He bares his teeth and is always ready to pounce."

"And the other one?" asked the boy.
The grandfather replied: "The other one has
it in him to become a pack leader.
He protects the young and knows where to take
the pack when the winds get too fierce.
He is full of love, hope, kindness, joy,
compassion, serenity and generosity.
He is peaceful and humble and has a great sense of humour."

"What do these wolves do inside you?" asked the boy.
"They fight each other for your soul."
"Which one wins?" asked the boy.
"The one who wins, grandson, is the one you feed!"

And so the feast of the soul begins with passion.
Let's eat!

"THINGS ALWAYS GET BETTER,
EXCEPT WHEN THEY GET WORSE."

CHAPTER 1

THE POWER OF PASSION

Ostriches have it easy!
If they want to ignore something they
bury their heads in the ground.
If only we could 'bury our heads' and avoid
what's going on around us -
the negative, the malicious, the demeaning,
the alienating experiences?

But that's not an option!
Only the naïve sing Pollyanna songs, share
platitudes, and bury their heads.
The "passionate" face ravaged relationships
with Christ's transforming love and
re-creating power.

Many of us would joyously return to our childhood where,
if we fell and scratched ourselves,
our mothers (if we were fortunate) would run and
pick us up with iodine and soothing words:
"There, there, it's all right! Things will get better!"

Then we reach maturity and discover truth.
Things can get worse, and often do!

Then, after further falls and scrapes we
discover the potential for **growth**.
We discover the presence of God.

We discover the sovereignty of God.
In "the pit of life" we find that growth is
possible as we climb out of our despair
on God's ladder, rung by rung.
Strengthened by the Spirit we develop new success strategies,
learning from our past and guided by the Hand of God.

We find God can indeed "turn our sorrow into dancing".
We find new hope and joy and, with the
joy, comes a new beginning!
Yes, things can get worse but there is always
the possibility of rebuilding with God.

How, you ask?
Because of our belief and trust in His sovereign power.

A wise counsellor writes: "Many of us are constantly
defeated by the circumstances around us because we aren't
ready to accept that the 'battle' is God's, not ours.
Even when we realise our own powerlessness
to cope with the enemy,
we are afraid to let go and trust ourselves to God's power."

Trusting in that supreme power enables us to deal
with our adversities, grow and rebuild.

Recently I visited a corner store which
happened to sell lottery tickets and,
seeking to start an easy conversation,
I asked the salesman if he had the winning numbers.

Then I encountered a modern secular philosopher, for he said:
**"No, I don't gamble.
I aim low and so avoid disappointment!"**

As I left the store, trying to digest that
insight, I thought: "Interesting!
That's how many contemporary Christians think
about God's opportunities and promises.
We've internalized that secular mindset!
We've become conditioned to 'failure avoidance' "!

AIM LOW!
Don't have any great expectations of God
and you won't be disappointed.

The only problem is:
YOU WON'T WIN EITHER!

The Lotto advertisement is true:
"You can't win if you don't enter."
If we don't enter a passionate relationship with
God and expect God to fulfil His promises,
that's exactly what we'll get - nothing.
And things will probably get worse!

As we stand confronting our challenges, this is
the terrible prediction of faithlessness....

EXPECT NOTHING AND YOU'LL GET NOTHING!

The audacity of vibrant faith is to expect great
things from God - yes, even miracles,
and live life with that sense of awe and wonder!
So begins the power of passionate faith!

We dare to believe God's promises based
in His Word are literally for us.

We dare to aim high in our expectation
that God will fulfil His promises.
We rejoice in His sustaining intimacy.
We know that God's response may not be on our timetable,
or in our anticipated ways,
but we base our lives on the fact that His promises are valid
and confidently live 'rock-solid' in that constant
state of trust and expectation.

We strive to anticipate the best, affirming with the Apostle Paul:

**"God is able to do exceedingly abundantly above all that we ask
or think, according to the power that works in us."**[1]

Naïve? In the world's eyes, of course!
But to those fuelled by the passion of faith, it is
the rock on which we build our lives.

No one gets through life without pain.
Woody Allen said, "Life is full of miserableness,
loneliness, unhappiness and suffering -
and it's all over much too quickly." [2]

AIM LOW!

DON'T HAVE ANY GREAT EXPECTATIONS OF GOD, AND YOU WON'T BE DISAPPOINTED!

"GLORY BE TO GOD, WHO
BY HIS MIGHTY
POWER AT WORK WITHIN US IS ABLE
TO DO FAR MORE THAN WE
WOULD EVER DARE
TO ASK OR EVEN DREAM OF –
INFINITELY BEYOND OUR
HIGHEST PRAYERS,
DESIRES, THOUGHTS, OR HOPES."
(Ephesians 3:20, TLB)

Norman Vincent Peale tells of meeting a friend in New York
who complained about his terrible life.
Peale said, "I know a place in the Bronx where
there are twenty-five thousand people with no problems."
His friend said, "Norman, take me there."
Peale replied, "It's Woodlawn Cemetery."

Peale's point is a compelling statement
because it's all about attitude.
Our lives may be difficult,
but our attitude will determine whether
that difficulty will defeat us
or elevate us.
Our attitude defines our difficulty!

M. Scott Peck writes:
"Life is difficult.
That is a great truth, one of the greatest truths.
It is a great truth because once we see this truth, we transcend it.
Once we truly know that life is difficult –
once we truly understand and accept it –
then life is no longer difficult.
Because once it is accepted, the fact that life
is difficult no longer matters."[3]

As Dr. Bernie Siegel says:
"What we can do is choose how to use the pain life presents to us.
I have people sit on my examining table screaming,
'Why me? Why did God do this to a wonderful person like me?' "[4]

In the movie HAROLD AND MAUDE,
Bud Cort asks Ruth Gordon:
"How come you are so good with people?"
and she says, "They're my species, you know.

If you are alive and a member of the
species, you will have problems."

So we move on and say, "Why not me?"
Then we move even deeper into our relationship with God and say,
"Examine me, O LORD, and prove me."[5]

We know that our trials have something to
teach us and we seek God's leading,
not for understanding, but for GROWTH!
Our example in this is Job who could say:
"When He has tested me, I shall come forth as gold."[6]

It has been said that
**"A successful life is not about NOT dying.
It is about living well."**

The power of God is at the centre of our faith.
It is manifest in the resurrection of Jesus
on which our faith is grounded.
The Gospel message is filled with God's resurrection power.

As "the Easter People",
we embrace the presence and promises of God with **PASSION**
and determine to allow Him to shape, mould,
and use us for His unique purpose.
The passion of expectant faith enables us to place
our "failures" into the hands of God
with the total confidence that He can make all things new.

**AIM LOW, EXPECT NOTHING, AND
THAT'S WHAT YOU'LL GET!**
But choosing to live with passionate faith will
bring rewards that elude all other options.

One of the most celebrated Scottish theologians
and preachers of the 20th century wrote:
"Today as never before there is laid upon the
heart and conscience of the Church
the burden of evangelism.
Other generations have their own specific tasks…

"Today the demand is more radical and basic.
It is spiritual resurrection: it is - under God - the creating of life.
To confront a bewildered and dishevelled
age with the fact of Christ,
to thrust upon its confusion the creative word of the Cross
and smite its disenchantment with the glory of the Resurrection –
this is the urgent, overruling task."

'Son of man, can these bones live?'

He states that there is,
therefore, no place today for a Church that
is not aflame with the Spirit
who is the Lord and Giver of life,
nor any value in a theology which is not passionately missionary.
If there throbs through the Church the vitality
of a living union with Christ –
and apart from this the Church has no
claim to exist, no right to preach,
it is merely cumbering the ground –
if the Church can indeed say,
'It is not I who live; it is Christ who lives in me',
then the dark demonic forces of the age have met their match,
and the thrust of life is stronger than the drift of death.'

A Church that knows its Lord and is possessed by its Gospel
cannot but propagate the life that it has found.
A Christian who is taking his life seriously cannot but evangelise."

These words shout encouragement,
and an urgent and timeless mandate down to
us more than half a century later!

The church must refocus its agenda and
seize again the priorities of Christ
in order to be both renewed and made relevant for our time.

Without that focus we lose transforming power
and are both cast aside by God and by the world.

Men such as this theologian were giants of the faith.
They stamped the church's moral and
spiritual authority on their society.

I grew up with such giants as examples,
where politicians would consult church
leaders before completing policy.

I ask:
WHERE ARE THE GIANTS OF FAITH FOR TODAY?
Where are the giants in our pulpits? Where
are the giants in our pews?
Where are the spiritual and moral giants in
our seminaries and universities?
Where are the men and women who will "turn the
world upside down" because of their passion?

Where are the "Easter People" who will unashamedly
stand up as transforming catalysts
in the self-destructive attitudes and behaviour of our time?
Where are the beacons of light and hope
rather than those who are mere mirrors reflecting current society?
WHERE ARE THE GIANTS OF PASSION?

Passion is the key!

The Quaker philosopher, Dr. Elton Trueblood, wrote:
"You cannot be a vital Christian if you are 'cool'.
The world, supposedly, admires 'coolness',
and has made 'cool' into a term of admiration.
Not so Jesus Christ.
He is saying that unless your commitment
is hot, unless it is passionate,
it has no relationship to Him.
Being 'lukewarm' is simply not acceptable!"[7]

As Trueblood insists this means that the Gospel is
not something you can take in detachment;
just something to think about,
The Gospel can be a matter of intellectual examination,
but if it ends there it is nothing at all.
He notes there is a world of difference between
detachment and involvement.
And Jesus is saying that it is passionate
involvement or it isn't really anything.
This means that the Gospel cannot be something you think well of;
it has to be something that you give yourself to,
and with all the passion within you.

Think of it!
No child was ever conceived without passion;
no great piece of music was ever composed without passion;
no great work of art was ever created without passion.
You can have a passionless Christianity if you want to,
but it will be without the Spirit and blessings of Christ!

Passion makes it happen!

The most striking metaphor used by Jesus
in describing His purpose is "fire".
He says:
"I came to send fire on the earth."[8]

This metaphor is presented in obvious connection
with the prediction of John the Baptist:
" 'I indeed baptize you with water;
but One mightier than I is coming…
He will baptize you with the Holy Spirit and fire.' "[9]

Now we have a rather strange corroboration of
Jesus' words outside the canonical gospels,
in the so-called Gospel of Thomas,
found in the dry sands of Egypt.
This Gospel includes the same words: "I
came to cast fire upon the earth."
Then there is this remarkable addition, for
which we can all be extremely grateful,
"He who comes close to me, comes close to the fire."

Down through the years the metaphor of "fire"
has been used to describe the revolutionary,
passionate, life-changing experience,
which Christ brings.
Charles Wesley describes this in his hymn:

O Thou who camest from above,
The pure celestial fire to impart,
Kindle a flame of sacred love
On the mean altar of my heart.

There let it for Thy glory burn
With inextinguishable blaze,

And trembling to its source return,
In humble prayer and fervent praise.

That's passion!

John Wesley picked up the same theme when
he used these words to describe his conversion
experience: "My heart was strangely warmed."[10]

When Blaise Pascal needed language to describe the vivid character
of his life-changing experience of November, 1654,
he wrote in large letters in his secret document, the word
"FIRE!"[11]

Vital Christianity is always passionate.
It has always been spoken of in terms of "fire",
where the individual becomes "consumed",
"set aglow", "ignited" by Christ.
Our old lives are consumed and a new life
and passion burn within us.

The Christian is alive and active as a blazing fire.
We embrace Paul's statement:
**"When someone becomes a Christian,
he becomes a brand new person inside.
He is not the same anymore.
A new life has begun!"**[12]

Such renewal throbs with passion.

Passion brings new birth!

It reaches out to touch others with Christ's
transforming power and love.

It's hard to read the New Testament and not
begin to realise that the early church,
in its period of greatest vitality,
was very different from most parts of the
conventional church in our own day.

Perhaps the most striking feature is that ALL of
the early Christians were missionaries.
They did not leave the evangelistic task
either to professional evangelists
or to salaried pastors, for these did not exist.

As we read the truly exciting story of the early church,
persevering as it did in the face of incredible odds,
we sense the difference between the task of
merely supporting missionaries
and of being missionaries.
The early church did not have a missionary
arm; it was a missionary movement.

Without that fire,
without that passion,
the church will not grow.
Theologian Emil Brunner was right when he said:
"The church exists by mission as a fire exists by burning."[13]

The only means of extending the fire is the enflamed, passionate,
individual Christian.
How else can it grow?
You can take a little fire here and take it over
there and start another and another,
and that is the only way to do it.

**The way you know whether anything is on fire
is whether it will start another fire!**
What a challenge for us,
because if we do not enflame someone else,
this means that we are not on fire ourselves.

We have all been staggered by the out-of-
control fires raging in California
where so many people have lost their homes.
It seems to have become almost an annual ritual of
gazing into the hell of that "fiery inferno"
as the wind-driven flames race through hills and valleys.

A man tells how one of his friends lost his
beautiful house in a terrible fire
some months ago.
His friend told how his house burned.
The houses on either side of his house did not burn,
but six houses up the street, there was a house burning,
and in the high wind a burning ember from
that house came through the air,
landed on his house, and burned it to the ground.
That's a frightening image, and yet that's how
the Gospel of Jesus Christ moves.

One person comes to have something new, vivid, passionate,
a life-changing experience, and then,
if it is really so, he or she cannot possibly hold it in;
they've got to touch people on either side of themselves,
in hotel dining rooms, on airplanes, in clubs,
offices, wherever they may be.

In the city of Salem, Oregon, there is a doctor who,
after serving in the war,

came to Salem and started a medical practice
with his wife and two small children.
And he wondered what he ought to do to
make his connection with the city.
So he joined the Methodist Church
because that seemed to be the most
respectable thing to do in Salem,
and he thought that it would be good for his
children to have a Sunday School.
But, he said that, of course, as far as he was
concerned, he wouldn't bother with it.
He'd support the church financially and
thereby be in good standing.

He could tell everyone that he was a member.
And he thought that was all.
And for a while it was all.

But there was a very astute pastor there.
This pastor, instead of begging the doctor to
come to church on Sunday morning,
which the doctor would not do,
began handing him books and got him reading.
Books like Bonhoeffer's LIFE TOGETHER –
the story of this man who left America and
its peace, and went back to Germany
and was hanged in a Nazi concentration
camp as a witness for Christ.

Soon this began to shake the life of the young doctor completely.
He began to see that he hadn't the right idea of
what it means to be a Christian after all.
It couldn't be a cool, detached, nominal, minimal thing!
And so his life began to change.

Now, every morning,
he gets up at five o'clock and, from five to seven,
he puts new religious books on tape in his
voice for the sake of the blind.
He has organised a prayer group of about twenty people that meets
once a week at his home -
a prayer group in which lives have been immensely changed.

There is a young woman there who suffered from
depression after the birth of her baby.
She found that people in this prayer group were praying for her
and she became better and is now a member of that prayer group.
This simply would not be true if it were
not for what the doctor is doing.

He has organized a family clinic in which
there are two doctors, two lawyers,
two ministers and two social workers.
They will listen to the complaint of any wife
against husband, husband against wife;
any parent against child, child against parent,
providing that the accused one is there also.

The result of this is that there are many loving homes,
when before they were homes of hatred and tension.

This isn't all that the doctor is doing.
This may be only a beginning of what he is doing.
But before he got on fire with the fire of Christ
he didn't do any of these things.
And the moment that he was really blazing,
he could not but make others blaze.

On John Calvin's crest there is a burning heart
with an open hand with the words:
"My heart I give Thee, Lord - eagerly, sincerely."[14]

Remember John the Baptist's words:
**"I indeed baptize you with water;
but One mightier than I is coming...He will
baptize you with the Holy Spirit and fire."**[15]

PASSION IS THAT BAPTISM WITH FIRE!

A missionary from Australia was visiting the
United States with her daughter.
After an evening service they went to do
some shopping at a local Wal-Mart.
The lights were blazing brightly all through the
vast store and the little girl was intrigued.
She picked up a flashlight, got some batteries, and turned it on.
In the middle of the lighted Wal-Mart
there was no visible illumination from the little flashlight.

So the little girl said to her mother, "Mummy,
let's go outside and find some darkness!"

**There's our mission in a child's words:
"Let's go and find some darkness!"**

To penetrate the omnipresent darkness around us,
we need the motivation and ideals of Christ's passion.
Such passion rejects out-dated church traditions.
It seeks to develop creative strategies which
touch the agonies and emptiness
of contemporary lives with the transforming power of God's love.

We stand amidst the world's chaos and affirm Paul's words:
**"Do not be conformed to this world,
but be transformed by the renewing of your mind."** [16]

Or, as another version states:
**"Don't copy the behaviour and customs of this world,
but be a new and different person
with a fresh newness in all you do and think."**[17]

THE WAY YOU KNOW WHETHER
ANYTHING IS ON FIRE
IS WHETHER IT WILL START
ANOTHER FIRE!

Too many churches have adopted the motto,
in their attempt to be relevant,
"Let the world write the agenda!"
That stance is hollow and counter-productive
to faith and the needs of our time.
We dare with passion to confront the negative strongholds
of contemporary defeat, oppression and decay, and
affirm Christ as the Light and Hope of the world.

Christ is our passion!

CHAPTER 2

THE POWER TO PERSIST

In the movie SCENT OF A WOMAN,
retired United States Army Colonel Frank Slade,
blinded in an accidental grenade explosion,
decides to spend Thanksgiving weekend at the
Waldorf Astoria Hotel in New York City.
After certain celebrations he intends to
shoot himself in his bedroom,
motivated by the total despair of the
meaninglessness of his blind and ruined life.

Teenage student, Charlie Simms, his travelling
companion for the week-end,
discovers Slade as he prepares for his suicide.
Simms tries to wrestle the gun away from the blind colonel
and persuade him not to quit on life.
Out of his abject despair, Slade shouts: "What life?
I got no life!
I'm in the dark here.
You understand?
I'm in the dark!" [1]

We can empathise with that emotional state,
either literally or symbolically.
In times of adversity we often quit, or think of quitting,
as we focus on our losses and the emptiness of
the future with its lack of opportunity.

We feel stuck in darkness and, in our pervasive
discouragement, we want to quit.

The word "persist" is not in our vocabularies at such times and yet,
for the passionate of spirit,
persistence is one of the golden keys to achievement.

For the despairing, how is such persistence possible?
By believing in God's plan and promises for our lives and,
regardless of our present circumstances,
trusting Him for continued guidance and strength.
When asked the secret of his success in
building the world's largest church,
Korean pastor, Dr. Yongi Cho simply stated: "I pray. I obey!" [2]

That's it!
No elaborate formula for success based on
ingenious motivational principles,
but basic obedience to the will and guidance of God.

Obedience is the key!
We passionately seek God's plan for our lives, then
commit ourselves in obedience to that plan, regardless
of the circumstances that come against us.
Quitting on God's plan and promises is not
an option for the passionate believer!

We base our lives on the "nevertheless" principle,
then move forward trusting God to guide us
and demonstrate His power.

I was always fascinated by the story of those three Israelites:
Shadrack, Meshack and Abednego.

These young men, living in Babylonian exile,
were commanded on penalty of death,
to worship the golden idol of the King.
In obedience to their faith, they refused, stating:

"Our God whom we serve is able to deliver
us from the burning fiery furnace,
and He will deliver us from your hand, O king.
BUT IF NOT,
let it be known to you, O king, that we do not serve your gods,
nor will we worship the gold image which you have set up. [3]"

Because of their disobedience to the king, they were
tied up and thrown into "the fiery furnace",
heated so hot that it consumed the guards placed outside.
Then there is the miraculous deliverance.
When the king looked into the fiery furnace,
he saw not three bound Israelites,
but four men walking freely about,
" '…and the form of the fourth is like the Son of God.' " [4]

This is the "nevertheless" principle in operation.
Note the process.
Only as the three men stayed obedient to their faith,
regardless of the consequences,
did God intervene and set them free.
So it is that, even if things don't work out the way we planned,
we hold fast to our confidence that God
is in full control of our lives,
and that He will ultimately work things out for our good.

Job had the principle deeply etched in his heart when,
under his awesome afflictions, said:
" 'Though He slay me, yet will I trust Him.' " [5]

The "nevertheless" principle is based on Paul's
statement to the persecuted church in Rome:
**" 'All things work together for good to those who love God,
to those who are the called according to His purpose.' "** 6

A wise Christian evangelist writes:
"The greater the blessings in store for a person,
the more determined will be Satan's attempt to hold him back.
Viewed in this light, as foreshadowings of blessings ahead,
our struggles can actually become a source of encouragement."

Over and above these factors, we are confronted
with the sovereignty of God.
God's perspective is different from ours.
He takes into account factors in a situation
about which we know nothing.

He always keeps His promises,
but in most cases there are two things
He does not reveal in advance:
the precise way that He will work in each life,
and the precise time that He will take.
We cannot dictate to God exactly how to fulfil His promises.
What we must do is maintain an attitude of firm,
unwavering trust that God will move when and how He sees fit.

The "nevertheless" principle operates through
our obedience to provide God's blessings.
Luke tells of Jesus' encounter with four
fishermen who had fished all night,
caught nothing,
and were washing their nets.

After Jesus had talked with them for a while He said,
" 'Launch out into the deep and let down your nets for a catch.' " 7

Here was a carpenter giving advice to professional fisherman.
Yet Simon replied, " 'Master, we have worked
all night and caught nothing;
NEVERTHELESS at Your word I will let down the net.'
(notice Simon's cautious response to the promised
blessing in letting out only one net,
and that probably was a rotten, unused net).
'And when they had done this, they
caught a great number of fish,
and their net was breaking.' " [8]

Obedience to the "nevertheless" principle provides
the opening for God to enter our lives.
When we strive in one direction, become frustrated,
and are on the verge of quitting,
the Spirit speaks to us,
calling us to do things in a different manner,
or simply to stand still in trusting faith in His promises.
This persistent refusal to quit,
suspending our need for understanding,
allows God's sovereign will to manifest itself.

This principle held true even for Jesus.
In Gethsemane, where He faced the awful reality
and dimensions of the crucifixion -
an event with which He was only too familiar living in Judea -
He was tempted to quit on His journey to the Cross.
In His prayer, so intense that he sweat blood, a
rare condition called "hematohidrosis",
Jesus said,

" 'Father, if it is your will, take this cup away from Me;
NEVERTHELESS not My will, but Yours be done.
Then an angel appeared to Him from
heaven, strengthening Him.' " [9]

Note the process:
only as He affirmed the passion of persistence,
the "nevertheless" principle,
did God release His strengthening angel!

If Jesus was tempted to quit, how much more will this be true of us.
His obedience to His Father's will enabled Him
to fulfil His mission of redemption.

Our passion for God, living with His transforming Spirit,
is what makes the "nevertheless" principle possible in our lives.
It enables us to break through the walls that oppose us,
empowering us to persist in striving for our goal.
Relying on our own resources destines us to despair and defeat,
causing us to lose our focus on the living Christ,
and sink under the waves of our negative state.

Focusing on Christ, however,
persisting in our passion for His Spirit,
praising Him for His goodness and sovereign power, enables
us to receive the blessings that would
otherwise elude us in our despair.
The "nevertheless" principle refuses to quit,
no matter the circumstance!

It is always a temptation to become dominated
by discouragement and quit!
But our strategy is to so fill our minds
with examples of God's power
and fulfilled promises that we will be sustained.

We believe -
The God of our history is also the God of our destiny.

This belief has the tenacity to face seemingly
insurmountable obstacles
with persistent courage.

As a counsellor of many years, I have heard
numerous despairing and tragic stories.
Men and women, experiencing failure, ruin or depression,
feel that life has lost all its meaning for them.
Out of their despair, they seek to quit through suicide.

Dr. Karl Menninger, the noted psychiatrist, said,
"People do not break down because they are defeated,
but only because they think they are!" [10]

Angelo Patri, a newspaper reporter in the United States, wrote:
"In you, before birth, was stored all the power you will ever need
to meet all the difficulties you will ever face.
Draw on it, encourage it; for if you do not use it, you will lose it.

**Instead of cursing life when things go wrong,
we need to realise that these difficulties of
ours have a propulsive power!"** [11]

Channing Pollock, the playwright, once said,
"People and cars go forward by a series of explosions.
A beautiful car cannot fulfil its function until
it has a series of internal explosions.
Just so the human being with conflicts and difficulties to overcome
gets somewhere and becomes someone." [12]

Here is the point.

We can never really make anything out of
ourselves until we get a few explosions into

the mixing chamber of our lives:
crises, difficulties, despair, hardships, pain, suffering, opposition.
These test whether there is anything to us or not.
If these explosions tear us to pieces,
we are simply not drawing on that power which
God promises to flow into our lives
at the time of trial.

When you are tempted to quit, remember:
the God of our history is the God of our destiny.
Recall the ways in which God has intervened
with power in your life in the past
and trust Him for the present challenge.

The famous violinist Paganini
was once performing before a very distinguished audience
when a string on his violin snapped.
The audience was startled, but the master musician, unruffled,
continued to play on the three remaining strings.

Suddenly another string broke.
Still Paganini played without hesitation.
Then, with a sharp crack, the third string snapped.
For a brief moment the artist stopped,
raised his beautiful Stradivarius high in one hand and announced,
"One string and Paganini!"

Whatever our circumstance we say, "One string - and God!"

There may be times in our lives when one
string after another will snap
and we will want to quit.
We lose the passion to persist.
It happened to Grace Anderson.

Her only daughter was killed in a car accident.
One string snapped!
Then her eighteen-year-old son died after a brief illness.
Another string snapped!
Finally, her husband died after a heart attack.
The third string snapped!

"But", she told her minister, "I've lost everything, but not my faith."
And she added, "My faith is enough to carry me on."

Whenever we are tempted to quit
and we begin to lose our passion to persist,
heed the rough, rasping, determined words
of Canadian poet, Robert Service,
from his poem THE QUITTER:

" 'FEAR NOT, FOR I HAVE
REDEEMED YOU;
I HAVE CALLED YOU BY YOUR
NAME; YOU ARE MINE.

WHEN YOU PASS THROUGH
THE WATERS,
I WILL BE WITH YOU;
AND THROUGH THE RIVERS,
THEY SHALL NOT OVERFLOW YOU.

WHEN YOU WALK THROUGH THE FIRE,
YOU SHALL NOT BE BURNED,
NOR SHALL THE FLAME SCORCH YOU.
FOR I AM THE LORD YOUR GOD.' "
(Isaiah 43: 1-3, NKJV)

"It's easy to cry that you're beaten and die.
It's easy to crawfish and crawl.
But to fight and to fight, when hope's out of sight,
Why that's the best game of them all.
And though you come out of each gruelling bout,
All broken and beaten and scarred,
Just have one more try,
It's dead easy to die -
It's the keeping on living that's hard!" [13]

It's a tragic fact - things can get worse,
no matter how bitter or tragic our present losses may be.
Life can throw even more negatives our way,
with the demonic aim of grinding us into the ground of despair.
We can lose "one string" after another,
with the possibility of the final string snapping too,
leaving us completely destitute.

But, remember, when you think "IT'S
THE END!" it's never the end!
There's the promise of God's purposeful and
powerful presence and He says,
" 'I will never leave you, nor forsake you.' " [14]

" 'I am with you always.' " [15]

It may seem strange to associate the "nevertheless
principle" with Rocky Balboa [16],
the fictional folk hero boxer from Philadelphia.
Born into what others would call "nothing"
and having little going for him,
Rocky begins his climb from the bottom
to being heavyweight champion -
fighting against the odds all the way.

But Rocky teaches us a lesson of passion
solely from the human point.
In the last movie of the series, Rocky has
returned to his old neighbourhood,
his wife has died,
he's lost his money,
and the respect of his peers.
Trying to regain something of his identity he
opens and operates his old boxing gym.

In this period of adjustment he is challenged by his son
who talks about how tough it is living in his father's shadow,
making a variety of excuses for his inability to thrive.

Rocky tells him how, when he was born,
he thought his son was going to be the best in the world.
Then Rocky says, "The time came for you to be your own man and,
for a while you were.
Somewhere along the line you changed.
You stopped being you.
You let people stick their fingers in your face
and tell you what you could do.
And when things got hard you began to
look for something to blame."

Rocky, who has consistently refused to make
any excuses for where he is in life,
despite the setbacks caused by others, continues:
"The world ain't all sunshine and rainbows.
It's a very mean and nasty place and I don't care how tough you are,
it'll beat you to your knees and keep you there if you let it.

You, me, nobody is going to hit us as hard as life,
but it ain't about how hard you're hit.

It's about how hard you can get hit and keep moving forward.
It's about how much you can take and keep moving forward.
That's how winning is done.

Now, if you know what you're worth,
go out and get what you're worth.
But you got to be willing to take the hits and stop
pointing fingers that you're not there
because of him, or her, or anybody.
Cowards do that, and that ain't you.
You're better than that.
Until you start believing in yourself, you ain't going to have a life!"

That's the success secret of the so-called "Italian Stallion"!
Rocky rose to incredible heights because
of his intense belief in himself,
in his inner passion,
with what sports analysts call "heart".

Rocky had the inner passion to persist.

How much more should this be true of us who have
the spirit of the Living God abiding in us, guiding
us, empowering us, to do His will?

There comes a time for every Christian when we begin
to understand that resting in the arms of
Jesus is what providence is all about.
There, free of all worry and fear, we are
able when "things get worse",
to continue to live in trust based on the "nevertheless
principle" and the victory it brings.

Olympic champion Bob Richards once spoke about athletic heroes.
He told the story of an Australian boy, Herb Elliott.
One day Elliott saw a man named John Landy
run a mile in under four minutes.
That's commonplace now, but a rare athletic feat at that time.

As Elliott watched Landy race down the
track at that incredible speed,
all of a sudden something hit him in the head
and it exploded in his mind and he said,
"I know I can run a mile in less than four minutes."

Elliott went to a man named Cerutty,
who was the most renowned coach in
Australia at that time, and said,
"Mr. Cerutty, I know I can run the mile in less than four minutes."
Cerutty answered,
"Son, do you know what it takes to run the
mile in less than four minutes?
You become so exhausted you could almost die,
and you suck in hot air until you're almost unconscious.
You can hardly stand up."

The young man persisted,
"I have a feeling in my mind. I don't care what it takes.
I want to run the mile in under four minutes."

That's passion!

"All right", sighed the coach as he looked down at Elliott's foot
(he was recuperating from a broken bone).
"Come to the track tomorrow."
Elliott was there the next day.

Cerutty did not put him on the track; he
took him out to a nearby beach,
ran him up and down the sand dunes
and over rocks and boulders hour after hour,
thinking the boy would drop in his tracks.
But Elliott continued to struggle on.
He wouldn't give up.

A year later, Cerutty watched Elliott run
the mile in 3:57.8 in the Coliseum.
Then he later ran 3:54.5 to smash the prevailing world record.

Was it because he had good legs?
Was it because he had good lungs and a tough heart?
No!

It was because a tremendous thought
changed him and changed his life.
That's what happens when a person gets a vision
of the greatness within and responds.
There isn't anything in the world that
God cannot do with you or me
if we forget ourselves and let this explosion take place in our minds.

Dr. Maxwell Maltz in his book PSYCHO-
CYBERNETICS maintains that our
self-image is the key to change, and he says,
"If you have a certain image of yourself, that is what you will be.
But if you get a different self-image, you can
become whatever else you want to be." [17]

If that's true on a human level,
how much more profound and powerful will
that truth be when we become gripped,

possessed, and controlled by the image of what God intends for us!
When we see ourselves through God's eyes,
gazing deep into the very recesses of our vast unlimited potential,
we become impassioned by a new and glorious
image of what we can become
through Him.

This passion motivated the Apostle Paul,
causing him to face life with single-minded purpose.
He outlines his passion:

"Not that I have already attained, or am already perfected;
but I press on, that I may lay hold of that for
which Christ Jesus has also laid hold of me.
Brethren, I do not count myself to have apprehended;
but one thing I do,
forgetting those things which are behind
and reaching forward to those things which are ahead,
I press toward the goal for the prize of the
upward call of God in Christ Jesus." [18]

Every person is grasped by Christ for some purpose.
Every person is a dream of God.
When we understand that,
the passion begins to build within us to achieve
that for which we were created.

Paul says he is "reaching out" for the things which are before him.
The word he uses is vivid.
It is used of an athlete racing for the tape,
with eyes for nothing but the goal,
with arms almost clawing the air,
with head forward,
and his body bent and angled to the goal.
It describes the man who is going **flat out for the finish**!

**Passionate persistence empowers us to
achieve God's dream for us!**

It has been said that the world has yet to see what God can do
with a person who is totally committed and consecrated to Him.
Do you have the passion of persistence for that assignment?

T.S. Eliot writes in THE FOUR QUARTETS:
**"What we call the beginning is often the end,
And to make an end is to make a beginning.
The end is where we start from."** [19]

I recall a New York pastor telling of visiting a
senior executive in his well-appointed office.
The office featured many fine works of art
but one picture occupied an important position,
even though it was simply a framed print.
It pictured an old wooden boat high on the shore where it lay still.
Both oars were in place, but they lay listless in the mud.
There seemed to be nothing more lifeless than
the picture of this beached boat.
But underneath the picture was the caption:
"THE TIDE ALWAYS COMES BACK!"

The pastor asked the executive how he came to possess this picture.
The executive replied that he had received it from his previous boss
who had displayed it on his own wall.
He said the man had gone through some especially tough times,
even facing financial ruin,
but he persevered in his goals and,
refusing to quit against adversity,
eventually won.

The executive said he kept the picture because
it reminded him of that same truth.
Whenever he became discouraged as he faced his own adversities,
he would look at the picture and articulate the title:
"THE TIDE ALWAYS COMES BACK!"
He received the same re-energising power to keep going.

Tommy Lasorda, world-famous manager of the
Los Angeles Dodgers baseball team,
kept this poem, "DON'T QUIT" by Edgar A.
Guest on the team's locker room wall.

"When things go wrong, as they sometimes will,
When the road you are trudging seems all uphill,
When the funds are low and the debts are high,
And you want to smile but you have to sigh,
When care is pressing you down a bit,
Rest, if you must - but don't you quit!

Life is strange with its twists and turns,
As every one of us sometimes learns,
And many a failure turns about
When he might have won had he stuck it out;
Don't give up, though the pace seems slow -
You might succeed with another blow.

Success is failure turned inside out -
the silver tint of the clouds of doubt -
And you can never tell how close you are,
It may be near when it seems afar;
So stick to the fight when you're hardest hit -
It's when things get worse that you mustn't quit!" [20]

"IN ALL THESE THINGS WE ARE
MORE THAN CONQUERORS
THROUGH HIM WHO LOVED US."
(Romans 8:37, NKJV)

"IF GOD IS FOR US, WHO CAN BE AGAINST US?"
(Romans 8:31, NKJV)

CHAPTER 3

THE PASSION TO OVERCOME

A humanist, loosely described as "one who lives
by his own strength and capacity",
would affirm this famous poem INVICTUS
by William Ernest Henley:

"Out of the night that covers me,
Black as the Pit from pole to pole,
I thank whatever gods there be
For my unconquerable soul.

In the fell clutch of circumstance
I have not winced nor cried aloud.
Under the bludgeonings of chance
My head is bloodied, but unbowed.

Beyond the place of wrath and tears
Looms but the Horror of the shade,
And yet the menace of the years
Finds, and shall find me, unafraid.

It matters not how strait the gate,
How charged with punishments the scroll,
I am the master of my fate;
I am the captain of my soul." [1]

This is a powerful testimony to countless individuals
who face and overcome potentially defeating situations.

Christians, however, move beyond that attitude to a higher level.
They acknowledge their own inadequacies,
then place their lives in God's hands,
and draw upon His vast resources to supplement
their own in their quest for victory.

For the Christian, Paul's injunction is clear and compelling:
**"Your strength must come from the Lord's
mighty power within you."** [2]

And again:
**"It is no longer I who live, but Christ lives in me;
and the life which I now live in the flesh I
live by faith in the Son of God,
who loved me and gave Himself for me."** [3]

Passionate faith enables us to overcome whatever
situation or individual would defeat us.
Faced with any adversity, we know that,
yes, things can get worse, but
"IF GOD BE FOR ME WHO CAN BE AGAINST ME?" [4]

Many of us have, at one time, had great
goals and dreams for our lives,
only to see them dashed and broken by circumstances
or the consequences of our bad choices.
It's easy for us, then, to focus on what we have lost,
whine over our mistakes,
and believe that our future is simply a matter of bleak survival.
We think we are too old, or too weak, or too wounded,
to start afresh in the adventure of faith.

Not so!

There are numerous Biblical narratives
which speak about how God uses
broken men and women for His purposes,
despite their years in the "wilderness" of defeat;
and made the second half of their lives
more fulfilling than the first.

Alfred, Lord Tennyson, the eminent British poet,
has captured this reality and faith adventure in the saga of Ulysses.
The Greek adventurer says to his followers:

"…Come, my friends,
'Tis not too late to seek a newer world.
Push off, and sitting well in order smite
The sounding furrows; for my purpose holds
To sail beyond the sunset, and the baths
Of all the western stars, until I die.
It may be that the gulfs will wash us down:
It may be that we shall touch the Happy Isles,
And see the great Achilles, whom we knew.

Though much is taken, much abides; and though
We are not now that strength which in old days
Moved earth and heaven; that which we are, we are;
One equal temper of heroic hearts,
Made weak by time and fate, but strong in will
To strive, to seek, to find, and not to yield." [5]

Add to this testimony of indomitable will and
strength, the mighty power of God,
and we have the passion to overcome anything.

I have always been fascinated by the spectacle of Niagara Falls.
In the summer, tourists and residents of that city are treated to the
magnificent torrent of water cascading over the rim of the Falls.

Some have tested their ability to survive the Falls by going over,
in a variety of inventive contraptions,
in such things as barrels of varying shapes and constructions.

But even more impressive are the Falls in ice-bound winter.
There the ice encroaches from either side of the
Falls in an attempt to stop the flow.
Yet all in vain.
The power of the water keeps on flowing to
power the electric turbines at the bottom.

This represents a picture of God's power working
through our oppressive circumstances.
The encroaching ice on the edge of the Falls well
represents our encroaching defeating adversities.
But the power of God cannot be contained
by such contractions and it continues its mighty flow!

As we live in passionate intimacy with God,
nothing can stop His power and blessings
from flowing in and through us.
That's truly a "Hallelujah moment!" and empowers
our passion to face the present!

A Chinese businessman in Hong Kong had
invested heavily in the stock market.
It was not a strictly regulated market and,
on one downturn, he lost everything.
A Western friend asked him,
"Doesn't it make you miserable to have had all
that money and then to have lost it?"

To which the Chinese businessman replied:
You Americans wouldn't understand.

Only a Chinese understands that when something is gone
the only thing to do is to forget it.
It is gone.
You don't have it anymore.
Don't say to yourself: I did have it.
You don't have it anymore and you go on from there.

At this time of writing we are emerging from the worst
financial crisis since the Great Depression.
This financial meltdown, with its vast job
losses and home foreclosures,
brutalized the lives of countless people.
It's here that the truth of the statement:
"THINGS CAN'T GET ANY WORSE!
SAYS WHO?" sinks in.
We listened to daily depressing reports as things
became worse for so many families.
So what do we do?

We are encouraged to develop our passion for God.
Tragedies strike us all!
Clichés abound, such as:
"Don't look at what you have lost, but at what you have left!"
That's true.
But such clichés are inadequate!!
We are told not to let our past, with whatever personal tragedies,
shackle our future
Our faith is based in this rock solid fact:

God still has great things in store for us!
If we learn to trust His guidance and harness His power.

He is able to take what we have left,
in material resources and intellectual ability,

and begin to rebuild our lives.
God will introduce into our lives whatever, and whoever,
are necessary as He opens doors to a new beginning.

The late President of the United States, John F. Kennedy,
a victim of war wounds, bad health and circumstance,
knew this attitude well, when he said:
"Anyone who believes there is fairness in this
life is seriously misinformed." [6]
Then came Dallas, Texas, November 1963!

Each one of us, at some time, will experience
the truth that life is unfair,
sometimes at great personal cost and frustration:
the unexpected tragedies, natural disasters,
the consequences of our own sin and
misjudgments, or the malice of others.

TRAGEDY IS A FACT OF LIFE!

When confronted with this fact, we can either whine or climb!
To climb,
we work with our abilities,
with what we have left.
As we develop a new goal, with a determined, creative response,
we overcome the adversity
through the unlimited power of the God of "new beginnings".

The passion of our faith powers us through adversities.
Paul's writings are filled with this passion to energize our faith.
Fill your mind and spirit with these affirmations on a daily basis:

"I can do all things through Christ who strengthens me." [7]

"God shall supply all your need according to
His riches in glory by Christ Jesus." [8]

"Be anxious for nothing,
but in everything by prayer and supplication,
with thanksgiving, let your requests be made known to God;
and the peace of God, which surpasses all understanding,
will guard your hearts and minds through Christ Jesus." [9]

When we face "impossibilities", listen to Annie Johnson Flint:
"Have you come to the Red Sea in your life,
where, in spite of all you can do,
there is no way out,
there is no way back,
there is no other way but through.
You have to go on if you are to grow." [10]

Yes, God allows adversity!
Adversity is used as the growing edge for faith people.
It's often the way He refines and sharpens
us for His unique purpose.
It took me some time, and some personal adversity,
to appreciate this truth behind Paul's "amazing"
statement to the church in Rome:

"Rejoice in hope of the glory of God. And not only that,
but we also glory in tribulations, knowing that
tribulation produces perseverance;
and perseverance, character; and character, hope.
Now hope does not disappoint,
because the love of God has been poured out in our hearts by the
Holy Spirit who was given to us." [11]

Scripture tells us that Jesus Himself learned from His sufferings.
Most of us can relate to that,
but rejoice in suffering?
That's a whole different level of faith!

A pastor who has made this principle of "praise
and thanksgiving" the core of his ministry,
tells of counseling a young drug addict.
The young man had made a complete mess out of his life
and was skeptical about the power of God to
change and heal him of his addiction.

But he was willing to give it a try under the
encouragement of the pastor.
The pastor said:
"Thank God right now for what He's going to
do for you in the next few minutes,
and thank Him for everything that has happened
in your life to bring you to this spot!"

"Now wait a minute!"
The young man looked upset.
"You mean I'm supposed to thank God for
everything in my life up to now,
even that I'm an addict?"
"It's your addiction that brings you to God, isn't it?" the pastor said.
"If God heals you, forgives you,
and gives you a brand-new, eternal life with Jesus,
don't you think you can thank Him for everything
that made you see you needed Him?"

After the man agreed, the pastor began to pray
in praise and thanksgiving for healing
and the work of the Holy Spirit in his life.

When the pastor finished praying there was a
strange new light in the young man's eyes.
"It's very strange," he said,
"but for some reason I really do believe that
God has taken everything bad
that ever happened to me and it's working for my good."

The pastor continued:
"What happened next, defies my ability to explain.
I placed my hands on his head again,
praying that God would heal him,
cleanse his mind of all desire for drugs, and
fill him instead with His love.
I felt a force flow through the young man.
His face brightened like a child's and tears flowed down his cheeks"
"It has happened!" he shouted. "I don't need
drugs anymore - Jesus lives in me!"

For that young man it was a moment of rebirth.
He would never again be the same.
He was born again,
not because he "felt" the presence of Jesus,
but because he made a decision to TRUST God.

THE PASSION OF THANKSGIVING OVERCOMES!

What an example of "rejoicing in suffering"!
It was the sincere ability to give praise and
thanks to God for his drug addiction
which set the young man free from its power.
Yes, it was a miraculous healing!

It's an application of Paul's unequivocal instruction:
"In everything give thanks;

for this is the will of God in Christ Jesus for you." [12]

"REJOICE IN THE LORD ALWAYS!"

There's a well-known phrase:
"God lives in the praises of His people!"
When we praise God for our lives, seeking forgiveness,
His Spirit is alive, thriving within us, directing us in our every step.

Passionate faith enables us to embrace those things
which are beyond our understanding;
to place our trust firmly in the sovereign
power and authority of God.
It's a trust which acknowledges that He always
has our best interests in mind.
God knows the complete and proper unfolding of our lives
and He moulds everything to fulfill His destiny for us.

With this faith we can affirm God's word to Jeremiah:

"I know the plans I have for you,
says the Lord. They are plans for good and not for evil,
to give you a future and a hope." [13]

Passion to overcome is firmly grounded in
our belief in God's invincible power!
We condition our minds with those Biblical
examples and principles of God's ability
to empower His people to overcome their
seemingly impossible situations.
When one door closes,
God gives the seeds of opportunity for
increased personal development.
We believe that, within the will of God,

such "closures" are our new beginning as God opens other doors.

We stand firmly grounded in our faith and trust in God,
fully believing that He is able to make all things
work together for our good and growth.
Rather than being bitter as doors close,
we look with expectancy for new opportunities.

The president of a United States steel company
made this comment to a pastor,
"Your business and mine aren't too different."
The pastor thought this rather strange
but the president's answer made sense when he said:
"I make steel FOR people, but you put steel INTO people!"

A minister told the story of the late Martin
Madden who, for many years,
was a distinguished Congressman from the state of Illinois.
It seems that a very brilliant young man
was also elected to Congress
and became a member of Madden's Illinois delegation.

Shortly afterwards, Madden, the veteran,
mature, philosophical Congressman,
a man of firm integrity,
became aware of the fact that this younger Congressman
was being motivated by special interests.
It was obvious to Madden that this
Congressman's votes in the Congress
were being based on certain influences which he well recognized.
He was concerned for the young man's future
for he knew well that a person with a shady
character would not last long

under the bright spotlight that shines down
upon a United States representative.

So Madden called the young Congressman
into his office and said to him:
"You know you shouldn't vote the way you did on this bill.
You know who is behind it.
You know the special interests that are involved in it.
Why are you doing this? Why are you making this mistake?"

"Well," the young man said,
"Mr. Madden, you realize, don't you, the pressures that are on me?
I want to stay in office. I want support.
Don't you understand the pressures?"

"Yes," said Madden. "I very well realize the
pressures that are upon all of us."
"But," he said, "Son, there's one thing you might think about.
Where are your inner braces?
If you do not get these inner braces,
you'll never be able to withstand the outer pressure."

These inner braces are formed through our faith
memory bank as we remember and use
God's power to overcome whatever issue
or situation would defeat us.
In order to achieve God's plan for our lives
we need to live in total dependence upon Him.
Our dependence never stops!

As one writer stated:
"God's power under us, in us, surging through us,
is exactly what turns dependence into
unforgettable experiences of completeness."

Paul wrote:

**"Not that we are sufficient of ourselves
to think of anything as being from ourselves,
but our sufficiency is from God."** [14]

There's this relevant experience from mountain climbing.
Imagine you're climbing a mountain far beyond your skill level.
And you're stuck.

Clinging desperately to meager handholds and footholds,
you find yourself unable to move forward or backward.
Your arms and legs begin to tremble uncontrollably.
You don't know how much longer you can hold on.

Then your guide, an experienced mountaineer,
reaches out and grasps your hand.
Your courage is bolstered by his reassuring voice.
"It's okay. I've got you.
Just grab hold over here.
Pull yourself up slowly. That's good."

Clinging desperately to his hand, you
eventually reach a secure position.
Drawing repeatedly on his strength, you
finally achieve the summit.
You know that without your guide's helping hand,
you would never have made it.
That's how we experience the Hand of God in our lives.
The Hand of God consistently comes into play
only for those who climb mountains.

A minister, early in his career, felt so inadequate for his new job
that the word he used for his state was
"plummeting" - falling out of control.

He sought the counsel of a wise Christian in his eighties,
a Bible teacher who had been a spiritual father to thousands.

The young minister said:
"I told him what I thought God was calling me to do
and then confessed my feelings of inadequacy.
I was trying to describe my crisis in some
detail when he interrupted,
'Son,' he said, in his kindly voice,
'that feeling you are running from is called dependence.
It means you're walking with the Lord Jesus.'

He paused to let me take in these words, then continued,
'Actually the second you're not feeling dependent
is the second you've backed away from truly living by faith.'"

The young minister said,
'I didn't like what I heard' and replied:
"You're saying that feeling that 'I just can't do
it' is what I'm supposed to be feeling?"

"Why certainly," said the old man beaming,
"That's the one all right."

The minister reflected:
"It's a frightening and utterly exhilarating truth, isn't it?
As God's chosen, blessed sons and daughters,
we are expected to attempt something large
enough that failure is guaranteed,
unless God steps in."

One commentator cautions:
"Success brings with it greater opportunities for failure…
Blessedness is the greatest of perils

because it tends to dull our keen sense of dependence on God
and makes us prone to presumption to
think that we can do it ourselves."

That echoes God's ancient warning to the Israelites:
"Beware lest you say in your hearts,
My arm and my power hath gotten me this victory."
How, when life seems to be overpowering
us and we feel like caving in,
can we apply Paul's words:
"I can do all things through Christ which strengthens me"?
For many people, even believers,
that's an incredulous verse, seemingly too good to be true!

The basic question is "HOW?"
How do we achieve the Promised Power?
It's the "HOW" most of us are interested in!
Given the mighty acts of God, few doubt the power of God.
He is able to do whatever He wills to do.
Certainly the God who created the
universe and controls the cosmos
can handle any challenge we bring His way.
We don't doubt the power of God
and we don't doubt the ability of God to
flow His power into the believer.

We don't doubt God's power but, what trips us up is:
HOW does that power flow into our personal problems?

It's more the practical, rather than the theological question,
of whether or not God has the power or wants to share it.
For years as a Christian counselor I've wrestled
with this application of God's power
to the daily traumas of my life and the lives of my clients.

HOW?

By following the advice of the Psalmist who wrote:
"Cast your burden on the Lord, And He shall sustain you." [15]

One may well respond,
"Yes, but practically, how is that done?"
For me the answer is found in that great passage:
"God resists the proud, but gives grace to the humble.
Humble yourselves under the mighty hand of
God that He may exalt you in due time.
"Casting all your care upon Him, for He cares for you." [16]

The answer lies in the difference between
the Proud and the Humble.
The first seemingly gives God control of their lives but,
when answers don't come quickly,
takes that control back and tries to solve the
issues in their own strength and ingenuity.

On the other hand,
the Humble person completely and consistently
places all his cares in God's hands
in the full, confident and patient belief
that God is able to do for him
that which he cannot do for himself.
Despite the length of time it is taking to solve
the problem, he still leaves it with God.
He believes, in God's time, the successful result will be achieved.
This person is the one who is 'exalted'!

I am encouraged daily, and I encourage others,
to follow Paul's advice.

His whole life was a celebration of the blessings
God showered down on him
as he struggled against all odds to build the early church
and leave the theological base for generations of believers.
Despite all his hardships and near-death experiences,
he wrote to the church at Ephesus from his Roman prison cell:

"that He would grant you, according to the riches of His glory,
to be strengthened with might through His Spirit in the inner man,
that Christ may dwell in your hearts through faith;
that you, being rooted and grounded in love,
may be able to comprehend with all the saints what is the width and
length and depth and height - to know the love of
Christ which passes knowledge; that you
may be filled with all the fullness of God.

Now to Him who is able to do exceedingly abundantly above all
that we ask or think, according to the power that works in
us, to Him be glory in the church
by Christ Jesus to all generations, forever and ever." [17]

What an inspiration!
Yet few of us really believe it,
much less internalize and experience it.
However, the faith-strategy of prayer and
praise enables us to overcome,
creatively responding to life's challenges.

Paul writes:

Now just as you trusted Christ to save you, trust him, too,
for each day's problems; live in vital union with him.
Let your roots grow down into him and
draw up nourishment from him.

See that you go on growing in the Lord,
and become strong and vigorous in the truth you were taught.
Let your lives overflow with joy and
thanksgiving for all he has done. [18]

With these principles guiding our lives we
are then able to say with Paul:
**"In all these things we are more than conquerors
through Him who loved us."** [19]

That's the passion to overcome!

I PRAY…

THAT HE WOULD GRANT
YOU, ACCORDING
TO THE RICHES OF HIS GLORY,
TO BE STRENGTHENED WITH
MIGHT THROUGH
HIS SPIRIT IN THE INNER MAN,
THAT CHRIST MAY DWELL
IN YOUR HEARTS
THROUGH FAITH;
THAT YOU, BEING ROOTED
AND GROUNDED
IN LOVE,
MAY BE ABLE TO COMPREHEND WITH
ALL THE SAINTS WHAT IS THE WIDTH
AND LENGTH AND DEPTH AND
HEIGHT - TO KNOW THE LOVE OF
CHRIST WHICH PASSES KNOWLEDGE;
THAT YOU MAY BE FILLED WITH
ALL THE FULLNESS OF GOD.
(Ephesians 3:16-21, NKJV)

CHAPTER 4

THE PASSION TO PERSEVERE

Morris West's novel THE SHOES OF THE FISHERMAN
tells of the election and activity of the first Russian Pope.
Shortly after his elevation to the papacy,
the new pope decides to dress as an ordinary priest
and visit Rome to become acquainted
with his people, since he is Bishop of Rome as well as Pope.

As he moves into Rome's poorer section,
he meets a doctor who sends him up into
a rundown apartment building
to give the last rites to a man dying of tuberculosis.

The apartment was a large, airless room,
cluttered as a junk shop and full of the smell of disease.
In one corner was a large matrimonial bed where a man lay,
fleshless and shrunken, under a stained bedspread.

His face was unshaven, his thin hair clung damp about his forehead,
and his head rolled from side to side on the piled pillows.
His breathing was short, painful and full of rales,
and a small bloody foam spilled out of the corner of his mouth.

In ten minutes the little tragedy was over.
The unrecognized pope said the prayers for the departed spirit,
while the young nurse closed the staring eyes
and composed the body decently in the attitude of death.

Then the doctor said firmly,
"We should go, Father. None of us will be welcome now!"

"I would like to help the family," the pope replied.
The doctor said very definitely,
"We should go. They can cope with death. It's
only the living that defeats them!" [1]

"It's only the living that defeats them!"

Millions of men and women across the globe
could echo those sentiments as they face
their debilitating circumstances, feeling cheated by life.

For years I have counseled men and women
from all areas of life who feel that way.
Spouses who have found their marriages
floundering through infidelity,
or increasing indifference as they have grown apart;
others who are in a financial and an emotional mess,
fragmented by the consequences of overindulgence in our consumer,
instant gratification culture.

Then there are men and women made unexpectedly redundant,
struggling to cope with little or no income
and the frustration of ageing,
and the pain of sending our hundreds of unanswered CVs.
They live with no job in sight,
but with a clear view of their diminishing
financial and emotional resources;
"Baby Boomers" with depleted savings and
inadequate or non-existent pensions.

There's the 'lost generation',
beyond the magic age of youth and without
creative, relevant job skills
(if such jobs were available),
caught in the limbo of uselessness,
with their noses bloodied,
rejected, and their self-respect as productive citizens ravaged,
wondering how "in their hell' they are going to survive.

There are the depressed individuals who
cope with failure and alienation,
consumers of society's most frequently prescribed drug "Prozac".
Theirs is not The Age of Aquarius,
but the Age of Valium
(and other non-prescription drugs),
stressed out,
struggling to meet their job targets,
fighting off younger, better qualified
competitors to simply keep their jobs.

Then there are the thousands who have
simply opted out of the mainstream,
having no reason to live, who simply crave the peace of suicide;
young men and women wrestling with the awesome dynamics
of struggling to cope in this unique age of unprecedented change.

To such people the concept of passionate
perseverance is an 'illusion'!

Yet that is the message of passion we share.
We believe that if we are persistent and diligent
in seeking and obeying God's will,
persevering in spite of every obstacle,
He will deliver the prize!

We insist that the person who persists
achieves what those who easily quit miss – their goal.
Here, then, are some of the essential principles
in developing perseverance.

Our focus fuels our passion!

There is no passion without focus!
Without intense focus there is no passion to persevere.
We will all face situations that stop us dead in our tracks,
seeking to deflate us,
enticing us to give up the struggle because
of the pain involved in persevering.
We're like marathon runners,
knowing full well that at a certain point in the
race we will run up against "the wall',
which has to be broken through in order to win.
Only the Apostle Paul himself knows the
number of times he could have easily quit
in the midst of his first century trials,
had it not been for his steadfast focus on the Risen Christ.

As the writer to the Hebrews states:
Let us lay aside every weight,
and the sin which so easily ensnares us,
and let us run with endurance the race that is set before us,
looking unto Jesus,
the author and finisher of our faith. [2]

Our focus –
"looking unto Jesus" –
is the basis of our empowerment to win
the race we are called to run.
We don't allow our past to shackle our future.

We believe God has great things in store for
us if we will simply trust Him totally,
and allow Him to guide us.
Paul again emphasizes the passion of this focus, when he writes:

Not that I have already attained, or am already perfected;
but I press on, that I may lay hold of that for which
Christ Jesus has also laid hold of me.
Brethren, I do not count myself to have apprehended;
but one thing I do,
forgetting those things which are behind
and reaching forward to those things which are ahead,
I press toward the goal for the prize of the
upward call of God in Christ Jesus. [3]

Can you sense the excitement, passion and expectation of his faith?
Despite unimaginable torture, ridicule,
the loss of position and prestige,
he exudes that champion spirit which carries him on to victory,
both here and in the life to come.

Paul's credo is:
I WILL PERSEVERE!
I WON'T QUIT!
CHRIST GIVES ME THE POWER!

Paul's passionate faith equipped him to face
and overcome every obstacle in his path
as he pursued his goal of full intimacy with Christ.

The woman 'with the issue of blood' knew
the power of passionate focus!
She refused to be blocked by her 'unclean state' which,
according to the laws of Leviticus,

should have excluded her from society,
and indeed opened her to the possibility of being stoned to death
if her condition was discovered.
But nothing deterred this woman from her focus of being healed.

She said,
and kept on saying to herself,
as is indicated in the meaning of the original Greek,
"If I can just touch his clothing, I will be healed." [4]
She was determined to stop at nothing in order
to achieve her goal - and she did!
She knew the passion of perseverance and the fulfillment it brings!

Are you facing a seemingly impossible circumstance?
If so, consider Lazarus.

Lazarus was Jesus' friend who died unexpectedly.
Jesus, rather than rushing back to console the family,
took his time in returning to His grieving friends.
Martha, Lazarus' sister, confronted Jesus for his
absence and apparent indifference, saying
**" 'Lord, if You had been here, my brother
would not have died.' "** [5]

However you interpret the story, the
following incident is fascinating.
In His divine power, Jesus ordered the people to roll away the stone,
despite their objection:
**" 'By this time there is a stench, for he
has been dead four days.' "** [6]

Then Jesus says:
**" 'Did I not say to you that if you would believe
you would see the glory of God?' "** [7]

Jesus called Lazarus out of the tomb and Lazarus, now alive,
walks out to be unbound from his grave clothes by his friends!
To say the crowd was "stunned" would be an understatement!

I say to people who live in their tombs of depression and alienation,
whatever their oppression might be,
locked up with their "stinking problems",
thinking their particular problem is unique and unfair,
to think back to the Lazarus story and see
the delivering power of God.
Realize you do not have to remain trapped in your tomb,
trapped in your past,
but that through God's delivering power
you can persevere through your problem and be set free!

As you persevere in spite of your obstacles,
believing in God's intervening power,
you WILL see the glory of God in your life!
This intervention may come in unexpected ways,
and at unexpected times,
for our God is the God of the unexpected.
But believe that His deliverance will come!
The Scriptures are filled with God's unexpected solutions to
"impossible" problems for those who truly live by faith.

A rabbi noted that the Hebrew word translated
"I believe" also means "I remember".
The issue for us when we're in the midst of our challenges
is to remember that that same delivering power of God,
which was active throughout the history of Israel,
throughout the history of the Church
and individual Christians of every age,
is available for us.
Stand on His promise of deliverance,
and see Him act in our favour and freedom!

Psychiatrist Scott Peck writes of the value of persevering:
"It is in this whole process of meeting and solving
problems that life has its meaning.
Problems are the cutting edge that distinguishes
between success and failure.
Problems call forth our courage and our wisdom.
It is only because of problems that we
grow mentally and spiritually." [8]

When we encourage the growth of our spirits,
challenging and encouraging ourselves to solve problems,
we grow through the pain and process of
confronting and resolving problems.

This is the strategy:
focus passionately and creatively on our goal,
or create a new goal,
then refuse to quit even when we are battered
and apparently blocked by obstacles.
Persevere even though circumstances seem so dark
that we cannot see beyond the seemingly insurmountable barriers.

Whatever the challenge,
keep on believing and trusting in God's
purpose and delivering power.
As Paul stated:
"We walk by faith, not by sight." [9]

Regardless of the circumstance we keep our focus on the Lord.
We are steadfast in our belief and trust in God
thus receiving the faith to persevere.
We persevere because we are grounded
in God's purpose and might.

Paul gives us this amazing promise:

" 'Eye has not seen, nor ear heard,
Nor have entered into the heart of man
The things which God has prepared for those who love Him.' " [10]

Focus fuels your passion to persevere!

One of the great motivational consultants of the twentieth century
emphasizes how crucial it is to focus and to persevere.

He says they are our constant requirements to
keep on fighting against the negatives
and ever-present temptation to whine and quit.
He tells how he's amused at these people who tell
him they are 'holding the right thought'.

I ask them, 'For how long?'
and they say, 'For a few minutes, anyway.'

He responds:
"You've got to get yourself in hand so that
you can **live** the right thought,
not just for a few minutes, but day after day."

Using the illustration of a tennis match he asks,
How far would you get in a tennis game if you
returned a few balls hit by your opponent,
then went to the sidelines and sat down for a few minutes,
then got up and started playing again
and returned a few more balls,
and went back and sat down?
It would be pretty silly, wouldn't it?

Well, the game of life is played all the time,
and to win you've got to stay in the game, whether you like it or not.
You've got to return everything that's hit at you,
with all the power you can put on the ball!

He says,
"Your opponent is **fear** and **worry**.
The only way to defeat him is by taking **positive, aggressive action**.
Stop trying to run away.
Stand up to fear and worry.
Look your enemies in the eye, make them back down and fade out.
When you face fear with courage, fear is through;
he's whipped;
he has no power over you
as soon as you throw him a fast ball with
'COURAGE' and 'I WILL' written on it."

This is the key point to note.
You can't be positive and negative at the same time;
one or the other must prevail.
Your head may be bloodied but as long as you don't bow it,
as long as you remain undaunted and unafraid,
you will have your enemy routed.
He can't retain any hold on you under those positive circumstances.

How do we find this inner power to persevere?
By following Paul's advice:

"Be filled with his mighty, glorious strength so that you can
keep going no matter what happens -
always full of the joy of the Lord,
and always thankful to the Father
who has made us fit to share all the wonderful things that
belong to those who live in the Kingdom of light.

For he has rescued us out of the darkness and gloom
of Satan's kingdom and brought us into
the Kingdom of his dear Son,
who bought our freedom with his blood
and forgave us all our sins." [11]

Recognize those things that block the energy in our lives.
Eliminate fear and choose to live with tenacious faith.
Unfulfilled potential will be unleashed and success will begin.
We all have to strive against fear and oppression,
but it is in that inner toughness, forged
through our alliance with the Spirit,
that passion to persevere is achieved.

President Theodore Roosevelt once remarked
that: it is not the critic who counts,
nor the man who points how the strong man stumbled,
or where the doer of deeds could have done better.

The credit belongs to the man who is actually in the arena,
whose face is marred by the dust and sweat and blood;
who strives valiantly;
who errs and comes short again and again;
who knows the great enthusiasms, the great devotions,
and spends himself in a worthy cause;
who at best, knows in the end the triumph of high achievement;
and who, at the worst, if he fails, at least fails while daring greatly,
so that his place shall never be with those cold and timid souls
who know neither victory nor defeat.

This is our affirmation: **"I will fight and not be afraid."**

Focused passion defeats pressure!

Don't be afraid of pressure!
Why?
Because **PRESSURE PRODUCES**!
Times of pressure can be profitable.
Life tests us, not to destroy us, but to develop us.
It's the pressed flower that produces the enchanting aroma.
The crushed fruit yields the tasty juice.
The fiery furnace yields the best steel.
Soil is rock that has been crushed, pounded and pulverized.
The pressure and heat of the earth's
elements create a costly diamond.
I like the way one person illustrated this truth:
"A diamond is a chunk of coal that made good under pressure."

The pressure to achieve meaningful goals is valuable.

Dr. Viktor Frankl, the Viennese psychiatrist,
schooled and moulded by the brutality,
personal losses and degradation of Nazi
concentration camps, insists:
"Mental health is based on a certain degree of tension,
the tension between what one has already achieved
and what one still ought to accomplish,
or the gap between what one is and what one should become."

"We should not," he continues,
"be hesitant about challenging man with a
potential meaning for him to fulfill.
What man actually needs is the struggling and
striving for some goal worthy of him." [12]

Interestingly, this psychiatrist believes that 'pressure'
holds true not only for normal conditions.
Frankl insists that in neurotic individuals, it is even more valid.

Using the analogy of a building, he notes that if architects
want to strengthen a decrepit arch,
they choose to increase the load that is laid upon it,
causing the parts to become more firmly bound together.
This pressure is the striving to achieve meaning in life.

The Greek philosopher, Socrates, stated this classic truth:
"KNOW THYSELF!"
as part of the crucial success strategy.
The way through the darkness, through personal difficulties,
is to be fully aware of our strengths and weaknesses,
then reinforce those areas where we are most vulnerable
and reach out from our strong base.

Recognize the tactics of pressure,
for this is a crucial area where the enemy operates!
The most important fact to note is this:

Pressure meets us at our points of greatest weakness!

We need to recognize our energy blocks.
Then break them down,
unleashing our full perseverance potential,
eliminating our fears, living by tenacious faith, until we succeed.
Therefore, we mobilize our belief,
based in the unlimited power and purpose of God for our lives,
trusting in His love and affirming:

"He who is in you is greater than he who is in the world." [13]

This strategy is similar to the process of welding.
When you take a metal object that is broken
and fit the two pieces together,

then subject those two pieces to intense heat
so that the molecules flow together,
that is welding.

Then, if you take a sledge hammer and hit the
repaired object with all your force,
you may possibly break it,
but it is highly improbable that you will break
it at the point where it was welded.
In other words, the metal has become strongest
where previously it was weakest!

Through the power of the Spirit within us,
our brokenness, our weak areas,
are "welded" together to sustain the strongest attacks of the enemy.
Where we were weak,
now we are strong and empowered to
persevere until we reach our goal!

Expectant faith in God's available power is
our ultimate defence against pressure,
the "forces of darkness".
We focus on God's purpose for us and, in His strength,
buttress our vulnerabilities and "the wiles of the devil."
We affirm every step of the way that:

"If God is for us, who can be against us?" [14]

Life gives no guarantees, except the reality of problems.
Things can get worse,
even when we feel we're at "rock" bottom!
Therefore, we increase our daily intimacy with the Spirit
and confirm our personal mandate in Him.
Paul knew **"…your strength must come from the
Lord's mighty power within you."** [15]

This promise is the basis of our passion to persevere.
No matter what, in the end God comes through for us.

He wills only the best for us and, when we
fully entrust ourselves to Him,
no situation, however dark or destructive,
can dislodge us from God's protection and power.

Paul found this to be true in his battle with
pressure - his 'thorn in the flesh'.
Though he prayed three times for it to be removed,
and perhaps was tempted to quit rather than persevere,

God refused Paul's prayer, saying:
**"My grace is sufficient for you,
for My strength is made perfect in weakness."** [16]

And Paul, infused and empowered by faith, replied:
**Therefore most gladly I will rather boast in my infirmities,
that the power of Christ may rest upon me.**

**Therefore I take pleasure in infirmities,
in reproaches, in needs, in persecutions, in distresses,
for Christ's sake. FOR WHEN I AM
WEAK, THEN I AM STRONG!** [17]

BE FILLED WITH HIS MIGHTY,
GLORIOUS STRENGTH SO THAT YOU
CAN KEEP GOING
NO MATTER WHAT HAPPENS –
ALWAYS FULL OF THE JOY OF THE LORD,
AND ALWAYS THANKFUL
TO THE FATHER,
WHO HAS MADE US FIT TO SHARE
ALL THE WONDERFUL THINGS
THAT BELONG TO THOSE WHO
LIVE IN THE KINGDOM OF LIGHT.
FOR HE HAS RESCUED US
OUT OF THE DARKNESS
AND GLOOM OF SATAN'S KINGDOM
AND BROUGHT US INTO THE KINGDOM
OF HIS DEAR SON, WHO BOUGHT
OUR FREEDOM WITH HIS BLOOD
AND FORGAVE US ALL OUR SINS.
(Colossians 1:11, TLB)

"WHATEVER THINGS YOU ASK
WHEN YOU PRAY,
BELIEVE THAT YOU RECEIVE
THEM, AND YOU
WILL HAVE THEM."
(Mark 11:24, NKJV)

CHAPTER 5

THE POWER OF PASSIONATE PRAYER

Have you ever been passionately in love?
You desire to be with the other person as much as possible
as you develop increasing intimacy.
Your spirit connects fully with the other's spirit.
You begin to experience that 'oneness' with the other person.

This is the background of the Biblical phrase "to know God".
Indeed as John writes:

"Let us love one another, for love is of God;
and everyone who loves is born of God and knows God.
He who does not love does not know God,
for God is love...
God is love,
He who abides in love abides in God, and God in him." [1]

As on earth, so is our connection with heaven!
Intimacy is the essence of prayer! It is
our communication with God.
We live in God's atmosphere.
It is the basis by which we are able to receive
all His blessings and guidance.

Jesus gave us the blueprint for this intimacy
in his "vine" illustration.

Abide in me, and I in you.
As the branch cannot bear fruit of itself,
unless it abides in the vine,
neither can you unless you abide in me.
I am the vine, you are the branches.
He who abides in Me, and I in him, bears much fruit,
for without Me you can do nothing...
If you abide in me, and My words abide in you,
you will ask what you desire, and it shall be done for you. [2]

"Abiding in Him" is the intimacy which must
be established and maintained.
God is calling us to be "joined with Him"
in order to "receive from Him".

Fear of intimacy and commitment
can prevent us from forming lasting personal relationships.
So it is with "divine intimacy".
But without that "abiding" we can do nothing!

Abiding in God reveals the faithfulness of God,
the truth of His Word;
and the manifestation of His promises.

**"God is able to make all grace abound toward you,
that you, always having all sufficiency in all things,
may have an abundance for every good work."** [3]

Our intimate connection with God releases His grace!

We focus on God, His Word and His promises,
knowing that God watches over His Word
to see that it accomplishes what He chooses.
We focus on God rather than our circumstances,
for such a focus shift empowers and sharpens our faith.

Focusing on our discouragements is self-defeating.
Focusing on the knowledge of God's love however,
releases the power of faith to operate within us!
Our discouragements begin to decrease,
while our "overcoming" courage increases.

**<u>Through intimacy we discover that,
while God is in the midst of our lives, we will not be defeated!</u>**

**"Being confident of this very thing,
that He who has begun a good work in you will complete it."** [4]

Sir Edmund Hillary, who attempted to climb Mount Everest,
lost one of the members of his team in the failed effort.
He returned to a hero's welcome in London, England,
where a banquet was held in his honor.
It was attended by the aristocracy and the
powerful of the British Empire.

Behind the speaker's platform were huge
blown-up photographs of Mount Everest.
When Hillary arose to receive the acclaim
of the distinguished audience,
he turned around and faced the mountain and said,
"Mount Everest, you have defeated me.
But I will return. And I will defeat you.
Because you can't get any bigger and I can."

As a schoolboy in England some months later I
recall watching his victory on a large screen
as he became the first person to climb that highest peak!

Abiding in God we say to our problems:
"You can't get any bigger and I can."

One of America's finest singers, Marian
Anderson, found this advice to be true.
Her early career was filled with such failure and
discouragement that she was shattered.
She was so crushed in spirit that for a whole
year she brooded in silence,
refusing every invitation to sing.

Her mother gently prodded her, saying,
"Have you prayed, Marian? Have you prayed?"

Marian answered, saying of that time,
"No, I hadn't prayed.
I embraced my grief."
Then, from my torment I prayed with the sure
knowledge that there was Someone
to whom I could pour out the greatest need of my heart and soul.
Slowly I came out of my despair.
My mind began to clear.

One day I came home unaware I was humming.
It was the first music I had uttered for a whole year.
When my mother heard it she rushed to me and
put her arms around me and kissed me.
That was her way of saying,
'Your prayers have been answered'.
Then my mother said,
'Prayer begins where human capacity ends'!

The result was the development of one of
America's truly great voices,
but it developed out of discouragement!

<u>Prayer begins where human capacity ends!</u>

Focus on God!
Live intimately in His Spirit.
Fill your mind with His promises of faith, not your fear,
for faith displaces fear.
Everyone faces "dark" moments, sometimes
for long periods of time,
but that faith-focus changes the future with an infusion of courage
revealing new opportunities for fulfillment.

Prayer manifests God's providence!

When Dr. Frank Boyden went to Deerfield Academy,
one of America's finest preparatory schools,
its future was precarious due to inadequate financial support.
Today it is a beautiful campus, with an
outstanding plant and a superior faculty.
When asked how he created such a school from
such unpromising beginnings, he replied:
"I think the banks in town had their doubts.
Probably they felt many times like writing us off,
yet, whenever I needed help it was always available.
I just kept on believing that we would come through."

Then he added:
I always believe in the law of supply.
When everything seems against you, and
when there seems little hope,
fill your mind with faith,
do your best, work hard, and put the results in the hands of God.
If you sincerely try to do God's will,
the law of supply will operate and it will supply your needs.
This school was built on that principle.

"And my God shall supply all your needs
according to His riches in glory by Christ Jesus." [5]

God's grace is beyond our understanding!

Grace results from passionate intimacy with God!
Let this truth become "flesh" in you.
Don't argue about it,
saying you will practice the principle when you understand it.
That stage will never be reached.
Instead, incorporate this Word into your life
so that its transforming power can be liberated!

Too many Christians have an "intellectual"
rather than an "experiential" faith.
They seek to understand rather than experience the reality of faith.
They choose to live self-sufficient lives
rather than living with a total dependence on God.
The result is that God is not real to them
because God does not have control of their hearts and minds.
They reject developing intimacy with God
through the Scriptures and prayer.
For such people Jesus' injunction, **"Abide in Me"**
is simply poetic rather than prophetic,
and the result is personal stagnation and defeat!

Jesus uses two rather humorous illustrations
to portray **the complete availability of God** for each of us:
the friend at midnight and the persistent widow.

Picture a typical one-room Palestinian house.
It is divided into two parts.
The main floor is used for family life during the
day, and as a stable during the night.

At one end is a loft where the family eats and sleeps.
At sunset the cattle are brought in and the
door is tightly bolted with a crossbar.
Soon afterward, the whole family goes to sleep in the loft,
the cattle settle down, and all is dark and quiet.

Then on this occasion, at midnight, when
everyone is sleeping soundly,
a persistent knock beats on the heavy wooden door.
Who can it be at this hour of the night?
Imagine getting out of bed, threading your
way through the sleeping family,
climbing down the ladder,
making your way through the cattle, and
then finally opening the door.

An old friend has come to the village and has no place to stay.

You invite him in and make a place for him.
Customs have to be followed.
The friend has to be fed!
Not only because he is hungry and tired,
but it is an unpardonable lack of hospitality to fail to offer a meal.
Eating was a sacramental expression of the bond of loyalty.
To refuse was to make an enemy.

But the host finds he has no bread in the house.

What will he do?
Surely his neighbour will help! Or will he?
His family has also gone to bed for the night.
What will he say if he is woken up?
The host has to try.

The scene shifts to the neighbour's house,
where the scene is basically the same.
The difference is that he has small children.
And parents know how long it takes to get them to go to sleep.

Regardless, the host has to get bread for his visitor.
All his urging is channelled through his fist
as he begins to pound on his neighbour's door.
Long silence.
"Knock again. They're still asleep," he says anxiously to himself.
Finally, there's an angry response:
"Who's there? What do you want at this hour of the night?"

Frankly, I really feel for the host,
caught between the demands of custom
and the reality of common sense!

"Friend, (for how much longer, I wonder?),
lend me three loaves of bread,
for a friend of mine has come from a journey,
and I have nothing to set before him."
There's a long silence and then the response,
" 'Do not trouble me; the door is now shut,
and my children are with me in bed;
I cannot rise and give to you.' " [6]

The neighbour turns over in bed, determined to go back to sleep,
but the children are now wide awake, the cattle too are restless.
The whole household is disrupted.
And, I daresay, his mind is filled with venomous thoughts!
Again the persistent knocking.
"What a neighbour!
He will wake up the whole village for three loaves of bread!"

Finally, there's no alternative than to get up
and give him the bread he needs.

We laugh - that is, those of us who don't have small children!
Then Jesus asks, "Well, what would you have done?"

We respond (piously),
"Why, of course, we'd get up and help the neighbour."

Then Jesus makes His key point.
If a man would finally respond because of his neighbour's need,
would not God, who **"is always watching, never sleeping."** [7]

Jesus says,
" 'So I say to you, ask, and it will be given to you;
seek, and you will find;
knock, and it shall be opened to you." [8]

**Passionate prayer for provision is based in
the utter availability of a gracious, loving Father!**

" 'If you then, being evil, know how to give
good gifts to your children,
how much more
will your heavenly Father give the Holy
Spirit to those who ask Him!' " [9]

GOD IS EAGER TO HELP US!

Jesus' second illustration is that of a dignified judge
who is having a difficult time keeping his rigid and hard reputation.

A certain widow is constantly bothering
him. He can't get away from her.
She's at his door in the morning, confronts him in the supermarket,

interrupts his conversation with esteemed
associates, disrupts his court,
and is waiting for him when he goes home at night.

The appeal is always the same.
" 'Get justice for me from my adversary.' " [10]

Now a woman, much less a widow, had few rights at that time.
If the rabbis prayed daily,
"I thank God that you did not make me a woman!"
we can imagine the general attitude towards widows.

All the more reason the judge's friends began to tease him
about his inability to get rid of this widow.

He is known as a hard, impervious judge,
who constantly refortifies his image
by protesting that he does not fear God nor respects any man.
But he meets his match in this widow.

The disciples must have laughed over the contradiction
between his statement of authority and his
growing fear of the widow's threats.
So the judge says,

" 'I fear neither God nor man,'
he said to himself, 'but this woman bothers me.
I'm going to see that she gets justice, for she is wearing me out
with her constant coming!' " [11]

The humour is found in a more accurate
translation of "wear me out".
Actually, the phrase is rooted in a bit of slang which means
"hit me under the eye".

Jesus is really saying that the judge is afraid the
woman might give him a black eye!
"Lest she come and beat me!"
is a literal translation of the Greek.

Once again, Jesus has used the "how much more" comparison.

If a persistent, scrappy widow,
who is a dangerous nuisance to a hostile, unrighteous judge,
can get him to rule favourably on her case,
will not the ultimate Judge of the universe
act on behalf of His people -
that's you and me - with justice and mercy?

Do you see what Jesus' humorous stories mean for us?
If God is so completely available to us, then
why not come to Him eagerly
and allow Him to transform our problems
with His presence, spirit and power?
It's an absurd waste to have such an inexhaustible,
available resource and not use it!

Peter Marshall, the famous preacher and
Chaplain of the United States Senate,
was fond of saying:
"God's way of dealing with us is to throw
us into situations over our depth,
then supply us with the necessary ability to swim."

No matter how deep the waters,
as we bring God with passionate intimacy
into our lives, He enables us to cope.

This is the experience of mature people of faith.
With such divine intimacy,
we are equipped to face that which has to be faced.
It may take time - certainly God's own time –
but the waiting period develops and tests our
intimacy before it produces results.

Roland Hayes, the Gospel and Blues singer,
tells how his grandfather gave him this advice:
"The trouble with a lot of prayers is they ain't got no suction!"

Pray with suction power!

How can we pray "suction-powered prayers"?
By driving the Word of God's promises
deep down into our problems,
allowing God's power to transform them
and lift us up into new solutions!
Our intimate connection with God drives His power
deep into our doubts, fears, inferiorities, and problems!
Pray deep prayers that have plenty of suction; the
result will be powerful and vital faith.

Peace comes from passionate prayer!

Researchers have studied the subject of worry
and they have determined that only approximately
8% of our worries are legitimate.
The other 92% concern past issues which
cannot be changed, health issues,
which only get worse with worry, and future
apprehensions which are uncertain.

**We waste time and energy, too often
worrying about the wrong things!**

I heard Ken Duncan, internationally acclaimed
landscape photographer, tell how he
battled for years with agoraphobia before he conquered his fear.
Out of his experience he said:
"There are two things you can do with fear.
You can either allow it to hold you captive,
or you can walk straight into your fear and, with
Jesus beside you, you can do anything."

There's nothing impossible.
Life is an adventure when you have Jesus.
It doesn't mean things aren't going to happen, but God is with you.
We are IN this world, but not OF this world.
We do not have to be concerned about the worries of this world!

Duncan challenges us:
How would you like to see a miracle in your life?
We'd all love to see a miracle, but you know what?

**To have a miracle,
you must allow yourself to be put in a
place where you need a miracle!
and allow God to demonstrate His delivering power.**

So many times we allow the wrong fears to worry us!

Duncan told of coming to the United States
to photograph the beauty of
the Denali National Park in Alaska.
He had heard of grizzly bears and their abilities.
They can run faster than a horse, swim very fast,

and can literally shake you out of a tree
with their immense strength.

After receiving instructions from the Park
Ranger regarding confronting bears,
Duncan and his assistant went off into the Park
and photographed some awesome vistas.

But as they returned to their mountain bikes,
they looked over and saw a large moose.
They got on their bikes as the moose began
to show a real interest in them.
As they tried to ride away, the moose began to gallop towards them.
With his adrenaline fuelling him, enough to win an Olympic event,
Duncan tore up the hill with the moose snorting behind him.
Then all of a sudden the moose stopped.

When they finally got back to the Park Ranger an hour later,
the Ranger said, "Ken, how did it go with the grizzly bear?"
Duncan replied, "Well, actually, we haven't
had a problem with the grizzly bear,
but we were chased by a moose!"
"Ah, the moose," he said,
"You've got to watch out for the moose.
More people get killed by moose than by grizzly bears."

The moral of the story is obvious!
We can spend our whole lives worrying about the grizzly bears,
when it's the moose that gets us![11a]

Only God knows all the factors that will impact our lives.
Therefore, we are called to live in this intimate
trusting relationship with Him,
and live within His peace.

Intimacy with God sets us free from fear
and worry to live in His peace.
Passionate prayer is based in this experience described by Paul
who knew personally the dangerous and
destructive challenges of the ancient world:

"Don't worry about anything;
instead, pray about everything;
tell God your needs, and don't forget to thank him for his answers.
If you do this, you will experience God's peace,
which is far more wonderful than the human mind can understand.
His peace will keep your thoughts and your hearts quiet and
at rest as you trust in Christ Jesus." [12]

The Psalmist captured the confidence of living
within the arms of God when he wrote:

**"Be still, and know that I am God;
I will be exalted…"** [13]

God stands sovereign above every situation and adversity.

Dr. Adam Burnet seizes this image of the unshaken,
exalted Christ from this incident during the First World War.
He was standing not far from the tall spire
of a village church in France.
For some peculiar reason the shelling on both
sides of the line had died down,
and in the stillness he watched the setting sun,
which looked like a great red ball of fire on the rim of the world.

Suddenly a single shell came screaming through the twilight,
and the top half of the church spire blew
apart with a deafening roar.

Almost simultaneously a flock of swallows
which had been nesting there,
rose excitedly above the smoke, dust, and flying debris.
They circled in the air for a moment,
and then settled back quietly on the
wreckage of where they had been.

Dr. Burnet said this reminded him of the greatness of God.
After the world and life are shaken, and men have done their worst,
God's greatness remains undaunted, unlimited and unimpaired.

Paul would certainly have identified with
this image as he wrote to the highly
challenged church in Rome:

What then shall we say to these things?
If God is for us, who can be against us?
Who shall separate us from the love of Christ?
Shall tribulation, or distress, or persecution, or famine,
or nakedness, or peril, or sword?
Yet in all these things we are more than
conquerors through Him who loved us.
For I am persuaded that neither death nor life,
nor angels nor principalities nor powers,
nor things present nor things to come,
nor height nor depth, nor any other created thing,
shall be able to separate us from the love of God
which is in Christ Jesus our Lord. [14]

Surely all of us would desire such confidence.
It flows from our divine intimacy!
Remember how Dr. Yongi Cho said, "I hear, I obey."
We listen to that "still, small voice" of the spirit and obey its leading.

Passionate prayer obeys God's light!

Speaking about the verse
"Walk in the light as He is in the light" [15]
one commentator said:
"Light is not just for seeing; light is for walking.
You cannot develop fully only by hearing the Word.

There's light you will not get until you walk in the light you have.
You will not get additional light in other areas
until you obey the light you have…"

"Walk in the light you have!"

We can go to conference after conference, take copious notes,
have everybody's CDs and DVDs,
but until we start putting into practice what we see and hear,
we will not learn the power of His presence.
So much of the light will not come just by seeing or hearing;
it only comes by doing.
As we practice the truth we know, the Lord
begins to unfold more truth to us.
You don't just talk about praying.
You pray.
You don't just talk about walking in love.
You walk in love.

Darkness includes confusion, ignorance, complications.
Many believers are confused,
but when you look at their confusion,
again and again you trace that confusion back
to the light they didn't walk in with obedience.

One wise counselor states: "The Lord leads us by steps.
He gives us enough light to take each step of faith,
and we don't require the light for the next step
until we take a step in the light we have already been given.

"Often the Lord has told us to do something,
but we don't understand 'Why?' or, 'What's
going to happen next?' or,
'How are we going to move after that?'
and we hesitate to obey.
This is simply a refusal to walk by faith!
Requiring the Lord to show us more before we'll step out,
is a refusal to walk in the light that we have."

Yet how many people would say, 'That's ridiculous.
I have to know more. I have to make plans, and so on.'
But they're in darkness.
And you won't get light looking into the darkness.
God requires us to walk by faith.
God will open a door.
He'll give us a direction and say, 'Do that!'
But if we ask for more information, there will be silence,
because we have all we need to walk by faith in the next step.

When we don't move we are in rebellion!

All we need to do is to take one step.
We don't need to see the whole thing.
Just one step.

The step of faith in obedience is all God needs to guide us.
Just keep walking.

One keen observer states that just because
you don't have light in one area,
doesn't release you from acting on the light you have.
Act on the light, the leading, the knowledge
you have, no matter how small,
trusting God to lead you to the next step.

Praying with passion releases power!

When we realize how much God loves us, just as we are,
no superlatives can describe that experience.
Just as magnificent sunsets,
or the ecstasy of intimate loving relationships,
elude description, so with God's love.
John writes:
**"Behold what manner of love the Father has bestowed on us,
that we should be called children of God!"** [16]

This love could only be demonstrated by
the self-sacrifice of God's Son.
When we see that sacrifice as being made for us,
showing us God's grace and forgiveness,
we experience the full Blessing He intends for each of us.
It's a passionate spiritual embrace based in God's promises to us,
releasing power!

Another devotional writer states:
"In our brains we have about two billion little storage batteries.
The human brain can send off power by thoughts and prayers.
The human body's magnetic power has actually been tested.
We have thousands of little sending stations,
and when these are tuned up by prayer
it is possible for tremendous power to flow into a
person and to pass between human beings.

We can send off power by prayer which acts as
both a sending and receiving station."

God is saying to each one of us who will listen and obey:
"I am ready to energize your life so that you
may receive new richness and vitality…
and through you I want to transform your community.
If you really knew what I could do within and through you
your ears would tingle with the excitement
and amazement of it all!"

"The effective, fervent prayer of a righteous man avails much!" [17]

Passion is focus!

This is the meaning of the verse: **"Pray without ceasing."** [18]

Not incessant words, but a complete and constant
openness to and focus on God's spirit.

Passionate focus means that every fibre of our
being is centered on God's promises,
committed to living in obedience to that
guiding "still, small voice" of the Spirit.
We stand on God's promises and,
even though we don't see an immediate
change in our circumstances,
we refuse to doubt and be "double-minded".

Our minds are fixed on God in complete
trust and expectant confidence,
knowing that if He has said something to us in His Word,
It will come to pass!
If we are passionate in prayer,

we will see our blessings from God grow and our
spirits overflow with 'joy in the Lord'.

Passionate prayer lives with audacious faith.
We expect God to do exactly what He
says He will do in His Word.
It is a complete trust in His ability to fulfill His promises to us.
Why limit God's activity to the area of our own understanding?

He is the God of the miraculous waiting, and eager,
to release that power into our lives NOW as we praise Him.

The faith that turned the first century world
upside down was not some anorexic,
emasculated facsimile of faith displayed by
so many Christians in our time,
but rather the vibrant belief in the power of
the living God demonstrated through
the resurrection of Jesus from the dead.
Passionate prayer is based on this audacious faith
releasing transforming power into every area of our lives.

Passionate prayer is trust!

Many people don't see God's promises manifested in their lives
because they become discouraged and quit too soon.
Just because we don't see anything happening
doesn't mean God isn't working!
Though the circumstances may look impossible,
our minds confused,
our emotions down,
doesn't mean that God isn't going to do what He has promised!

God is faithful to His Word!
If we will do our part and believe,
even though it's hard and others try to discourage us,
God promises that in due season, at the right time,
He will bring His promises to pass!

It may not happen as we expect or on our timetable,
but God is a faithful God, and He will not let us down.

God says:
" 'I will never leave you nor forsake you.'
So we may boldly say:
'The LORD is my helper; I will not fear.
What can man do to me?' " [19]

God will always make a way even though there seems to be no way.
He will give us strength for any battle,
wisdom for every decision,
peace that passes understanding.
And so we dare to trust Him, for He says He
"shall give you the desires of your heart." [20]

God holds us in the palm of His hand and nothing can dislodge us!

The Amplified translation states God's words:
**"I will not, I will not, I will not ever fail you,
or release my hold on you."**

This is the only place in Scripture where
God says something three times,
perhaps because He knows how easy it is
for us to give up on His promises!
God knows the pressures we face
and that's why He repeats this assurance three times.

We need to develop an unshakeable confidence
that what He says is true;
that we are not going to be defeated by our present circumstances;
or the length of time the manifestation takes.

We choose to magnify God's promises, not our problems!
We believe that God will show up with His delivering power.
God is obligated to bring to pass what He has promised!
Instead of complaining,
know that God responds to His own word.
God is always faithful to His Word!

We know that God cannot break His promises and,
in the face of our current situations, we say:
"Let God be true and every man a liar." [21]

"TRUST IN THE LORD WITH
ALL YOUR HEART...
AND LEAN NOT ON YOUR
OWN UNDERSTANDING;
IN ALL YOUR WAYS
ACKNOWLEDGE HIM, AND HE
SHALL DIRECT YOUR PATHS."
(Proverbs 3:5-6, NKJV)

A young minister and his friend went fishing in the Gulf of Mexico.
As they left the dock they asked the boat
owner how they would get back,
being strangers to the area, from their fishing
spot near some gas wells in the Gulf.
The boat owner replied,
"Wherever you are, just head back 'due north',
and you'll get right back to the dock."

So these young men travelled about an
hour or so and began fishing.
Suddenly a thick fog bank closed in totally around them.
The sun had set and it was getting dark.
As they finished the question was:
which direction should they take to return to the dock?
All they could see was fog.
Visibility was only a few feet around the boat.
Each of them came up with a different direction to follow.

Confused by it all,
the young minister got out his compass and saw that 'due north',
as the boat owner had said,
was totally different from either of their direction ideas.
Everything within both young men said
they were going the wrong way.
However, he kept hearing the owner's voice,
"If you go 'due north' you'll get back to this place."

Because of the fog they had to travel slowly.
It was impossible to see anything.
Time passed and his friend began to panic,
and he wondered himself if it was indeed the right direction.
Two hours went by and they were nearly out of gas.

Finally, when they were nearly totally in
despair, the dock lights emerged.
They were exactly at the place where the
boat owner said they would be!

Sometimes in our lives the fog sets in and every
voice in and around us is saying that
God's promises are unrealistic and the situation is impossible.
But, "Let God be true and every man a liar!"
In the foggy seasons, keep trusting God's promises,
and they will bring you home safely every time.
It may not look like it,
and it may be against our logic and emotions.
But we determine to dig our heels in and say:
"God, I'm going to keep believing you are in
control and you'll never let me down!"

God's answers are often disguised!

When Moses led the Israelites through the wilderness
they were totally dependent on God for everything.
God never once let them down, despite their
complaining and disobedience.
If God didn't feed them, they would starve to death.
When they prayed asking God for bread,
bread came every morning.
When the dew fell, the bread appeared.
God told them that the bread would come in the morning.
But when they came out of their tents and looked at it,
they saw what the Bible called "a round hoary
thing" that tasted of coriander seed.
It didn't look like what they thought it was going to look like
and so they said,
" '...a small round substance...'What is it?' " [22]

"Manna".
The word "Manna" means "What is it?"

We pray with passion for some solution to our issues
and yet God's answers may look quite different
from the answers we expected.

Instead of saying "Thank you, Lord" for the answer,
we look at "the answer" and say,
"Manna. What is it?

For example, you might be praying for a partner in life.
You say, "Lord, if I could have a good partner, I could make it."
Then you picture in your mind exactly what you
meant when you said a "good partner".
You had designed exactly what your partner
was going to look like, talk and act like.

God said, "All right, I'm going to send you a good partner."
But when you woke up and saw what God had sent,
you said, "Manna. What is it?"

Or you prayed, "Lord, make me the man I'm supposed to be."
So, God put you on a job to make you
the man you're supposed to be.
But when you got on the job you said, "Manna. What is it?"

We have to be humble in our prayers enough to say,
"If God sent it, I'll taste it and enjoy it.
rather than examining and questioning what I ought to be eating."
God sent down bread of heaven and they
examined it and refused to eat it,
but it was the true bread!

God's answers are largely unrecognizable!

This is where passionate trust reinforces
our commitment to the Lord
and enables us to receive His blessings.
Often God sends His answers disguised as problems
and we have to tear the problem apart to find the blessing.

Moses sent twelve spies into the Promised Land
and most of them came back and said,
" 'There we saw the giants…
We are not able to go up against the people,
for they are stronger than we.' " [23]

But two came back and said,
" 'He will bring us safely into the land and give it to us…
For they are but bread for us to eat!' " [24]

It's curious how twelve people can be in the same situation
and yet handle and perceive it quite differently.
One group sees it as impossible, while the
other group is eager to possess it.
Joshua and Caleb rent their garments and said,
" 'Let us go up at once and possess it'…
for we are well able to conquer it!' " [25]

The majority of the spies saw the "wrapping", but not the "bread".
What separates leaders from followers is
how they perceive problems.
Followers perceive problems as impossible;
leaders perceive problems as "bread".

Joshua and Caleb said,
"They're wrong. This is not a problem. It's bread!"

As we grow in intimacy with the Lord and pray for "answers",
He'll often send problems.
The challenge is: when we get the problem,
don't walk away from it and say, "Manna. What is it?"

Rather, trust God's process!
Tear the problem apart because somewhere, up under that problem,
God's got an answer for us.
Don't walk away from the problem, because
if we walk away from the problem,
we walk away from the "answer".
Rip the problem apart and get the answer!

This unshaken confidence in the faithfulness of God,
developed through our daily intimate time
with Him, empowers us to live with this faith:

**"All things work together for good to those who love God,
to those who are the called according to His purpose."** [26]

PASSION FOR THE 'ULTIMATE' PRAYER!

The prayer that challenges audacious faith is Jesus' promise:
Have faith in God.
For assuredly, I say to you, whoever says to this mountain,
'Be removed and be cast into the sea, and
does not doubt in his heart,
but believes that those things he says will be done,
he will have whatever he says.
Therefore I say to you, whatever things you ask when you pray,
believe that you receive them, and you will have them.' [27]

John puts the key point slightly differently:
" 'Now this is the confidence that we have in Him,

that if we ask anything according to His will, He hears us.
And if we know that He hears us, whatever we ask,
we know that we have the petitions that we have asked of Him.' " [28]

Many Christians always seem to seek a way
out from this audacious faith!
They think: It's just too amazing to be taken at face value.
Only an uncritical Pollyanna Christian would believe this promise!
And yet Jesus' promise holds the key to our fullest blessing.

Apart from the amazing promise itself,
our current mentality wants to see answers NOW.
But in the context of Jesus' 'cursing the fig tree',
it should be noted that even with Jesus
there was a twenty-four hour time span
between His speaking to the fig tree
and the manifestation of His prophecy.

Certainly in His ministry healings were immediate,
as was the miracle of stilling the storm.
But not in this instance.

The challenge for us is that we speak to our "mountain" in faith,
believing that we will receive our desired end,
and then we stand firmly rooted in faith in full confidence,
until the desired end is manifested.

Too many of us quit because the process is taking too long!
But the process begins at the root and demands time.

Regardless of the circumstances surrounding our prayer, we
"have faith in God"
and His promise, convinced it will come to
pass no matter how long it takes.

We call "**those things which do not exist as though they did**" [29]
and stand firm,
grounded in the belief that we will receive
the desired manifestation!
Whatever the "mountain" to which we speak,
we expect that through the power of God, activated by our faith,
the "mountain" will move!

Of course the cynic will laugh at such a belief,
but there are few areas of faith beyond the cynic's laughter!

Mature faith refuses to be undermined by
human perception or understanding,
Rather, standing on God's Word,
we believe the promise of passionate prayer will be manifest!

We believe that we receive.
In our prayer we take the promised answer
and refuse to allow any doubt
or contrary emotion to talk us out of our blessing!
We stand in faith and wait for the answer.

CHAPTER 6

PASSION FOR THE POSSIBLE!

The date was January 12th, 2010 when the
impoverished and tragic nation of Haiti
was devastated by a horrendous earthquake,
killing thousands and leaving millions homeless.
The resulting starvation and disease were catastrophic
and concerned people around the world
sought to help that desperate nation.

The question was "How?"
"What was possible?"
When confronted by a disaster on such a scale many people said,
"What can we do? It's too big and I'm too small."
And so they were limited by their limitations,
rather than being propelled by the possibilities.

Charlie Simpson, a seven-year-old boy from
West London, in the United Kingdom,
saw the catastrophe and aimed to raise $1,000.00
for the Haitian earthquake relief effort
through a sponsored bike ride
for 5 miles (8K) around the park near his home.

What can one person do?
This seven-year-old boy ended up raising well
over $200,000.00 in just two weeks!
How did he do it?

His call for support touched the hearts of people around the world
after he put a message on the JustGiving website.
On his JustGiving page, Charlie wrote:
"I want to do a sponsored bike ride for Haiti
because there was a big earthquake
and loads of people have lost their lives.
I want to raise some money to buy food, water
and tents for everyone in Haiti."

Along with donations,
Charlie was flooded with messages of
support from around the world.
One donor said, "Well done, Charlie -
you're an inspiration to us all."
A donor from New Zealand described his
ride as "an awesome act of kindness".
Another donor said, "We're cheering you on from Hong Kong."

One idea from a seven-year-old boy with a passion to help others,
plus the power of the internet,
touched the hearts of people around the world.
Charlie's idea of a sponsored ride grew from a "little seed"
into something so much bigger.

UK Prime Minister, Gordon Brown, in his
Downing Street posting on Twitter, stated:
"I am amazed by the response to the great
fundraising efforts of a seven-year-old."

Charlie's mother was amazed by the response as well, saying,
"We put it on the Web and that was it.
It suddenly took off and we can't believe it."

His bold innovative gesture showed that he
connected with what children his own age
must have been going through in Haiti,
and that he is wise enough to know that he can help them![a]

He had a passion for the possible!

Speaking at his brother Robert's televised
funeral at St. Patrick's Cathedral
in New York City in the late 1960s,
the late Senator Ted Kennedy said to all of us,
"It's a revolutionary world we live in;
and this generation at home and around the world,
has had thrust upon it a greater burden of responsibility
than any generation that has ever lived.

"Some believe there is nothing that one man or one woman can do
against the enormous array of the world's ills.
Yet many of the world's great movements, of thought and action,
have flowed from the work of a single man.

"A young monk began the Protestant Reformation.
A young general extended an empire from
Macedonia to the borders of the world.
A young woman reclaimed the territory of France,
and it was a young Italian explorer who discovered the New World.

"These people moved the world and so can we all.
Few of us will have the greatness to bend history itself,
but each of us can work to change a small portion of events,
and in the total of all those events will be
written the history of this generation.

"Each time a person stands for an ideal,
or acts to improve the condition of others,
or strikes out against injustice,
he sends forth a tiny ripple of hope,
and crossing each other form a million
different centers of energy and daring,
those ripples build a current that can
sweep down the mightiest walls
of oppression and injustice.

"Few are willing to brave the disapproval of their fellows,
the censure of their colleagues, the wrath of society.
Moral courage is a rarer commodity than
bravery in battle or great intelligence.
Yet it is the one essential, vital quality for
those who seek to change a world
that yields most painfully to change.
I believe that in this generation those with the
courage to enter the moral conflict
will find themselves with companions in every corner of the globe."

These are prophetic words for us in the 21st century!

"For the fortunate among us," said Kennedy,
"there is the temptation to follow the easy and familiar paths
of personal ambition and financial success
so grandly spread before those
who enjoy the privilege of education.

But that is not the road history has marked out for us.
Like it or not, we live in times of danger and uncertainty.
But they are also more open to the creative
energy of men and women
than any other time in history.

All of us will ultimately be judged
and as the years pass we will surely judge ourselves,
on the effort we have contributed to building a new world society
and the extent to which our ideals and goals have shaped that effort.

"The future does not belong to those who are content with today,
apathetic toward common problems and their fellow man alike,
timid and fearful in the face of new ideas and bold projects.
Rather it will belong to those who blend vision, reason and courage
in a personal commitment to the ideals
and great enterprises of society.

"Our future lies beyond our vision, but it is
not completely beyond our control.
It is the shaping impulse of America
that neither fate nor nature nor the irresistible tides of history,
but the work of our own hands, matched to reason and principle,
that will determine our destiny.
There is pride in that, even arrogance, but
there is also experience and truth.
In any event, it is the only way we can live.

"This is the way he lived.
My brother need not be idealized,
or enlarged in death beyond what he was in life,
to be remembered simply as a good and decent man,
who saw wrong and tried to right it, saw
suffering and tried to heal it,
saw war and tried to stop it.

"As my brother said many times, in many parts of this nation,
to those he touched and those who sought to touch him:

'Some men see things as they are,
and say 'Why?'

**I dream things that never were,
and say 'Why not?'**

This is the faith of those who, grounded in Christ,
have a passion for the possible and,
whatever their circumstance, or personal limitation, affirm:

"With God all things are possible!" [1]

Passionate faith seeks to transform
ourselves into a likeness of Christ
and our communities into places of justice, equality and love.
These are unrealistic and naïve goals, say
the cynical and self-centered.
But for us, who 'abide in Christ', this is
the dynamic that fuels our lives.

In this quest for a greater manifestation of Christ's
spirit in our lives and communities,
we are inspired by the faith of those Haitian Christians who,
in the face of their devastation, affirmed
their faith in the Lord who said:

**" 'In the world you will have tribulation,
but be of good cheer, I have overcome the world.' "** [2]

Some two weeks after the earthquake,
despite all they had lost and the suffering they endured,
Haitians opened their own pockets at this church
service to help their fellow citizens.
At the regular Sunday service at the Auditorium
of the Church of Christ of Port-au-Prince,
members dropped tightly folded precious Haitian dollars
into black plastic bags used as collection plates.

Too afraid to enter their beloved church,
worshippers stood instead on the street
in the shade of the massive church building,
with deep cracks appearing in its walls.
A few sat on plastic chairs, thumbing through well-worn Bibles.
They prayed for those they had lost.
Shoes were pristinely polished, shirts pressed,
ties miraculously found in the debris.
Bows, ribbons, hats adorned women's hair.

The congregation which, in normal times numbers about 1300,
lost members and a minister in the earthquake.
One hundred men, women, and children gathered for this service.
In perfect harmony they sang, eyes closed,
faces turned to the clear blue sky:

**"My shelter is in you, my
heart will always sing for you,
Because you deliver me, and
every time I'm afraid, I depend
On you,
And in my weakness, God
makes me strong."**

King David certainly knew what it was
to be assaulted and devastated,
time and again in his life,
even though he had been anointed by God.
He continually encouraged himself in the Lord and maintained:
"I have pitched my tent in the land of hope." [3]

When you face impossible situations
draw encouragement from David's faith and experience.
One crucial illustration of this occurred at a place called Ziglag.

David and his army had been away from their camp and
when they returned found the camp completely
devastated by an invading tribe.
The invaders had taken all their possessions,
their women and children,
then burned what was left.

Exhausted, they now faced devastation.
In their emotional despair they considered
killing their leader, David.
How did David handle this personal attack?
By being passionate about the possible!
The Scripture says:
"David strengthened himself in the LORD his God." [4]

And the Lord led David to recapture everything they had lost.

Passion for the possible, no matter what the situation,
always seeks 'encouragement and guidance from the Lord'.
We stand firm in the power of God, holding fast to Hope.
When everything around us is crumbling and shaking,
we affirm God's word to Jeremiah:
**"I know the plans I have for you…
They are plans for good and not for evil,
to give you a future and a hope."** [5]

"God will make a way where there seems to be no way!"

When the movie "The Seventh Seal" by Ingmar Bergman
was shown in 1958 in New York City,
Bobby Fisher, who had just won the world chess
championship, was in the audience.
The movie is built around the story of a medieval knight
who is playing a game of chess with the Prince of Darkness.

All the way through the movie,
the Prince of Darkness is making moves on
the knight, trying to trap him.

And in the last scene, the Prince of Darkness
makes a move on the chessboard,
looks at the knight, and says, "Checkmate!"
The game is over!
The Prince of Darkness - the Devil - has won!
And the curtain comes down.

Bobby Fisher is reported to have turned to his friend and said,
"Why is the knight giving up? Doesn't he see it?
Doesn't he see the pieces on the board?
The King has one more move! He can win!
The King has one more move!"

<u>"The King has one more move!"</u>

What an impact this has in our lives!

No matter how devastating the circumstance,
however impossible our current situation,
God is still able to enter and enable us to see new possibilities.
His purpose can still be made real within us.
He challenges us to look beyond our failures,
inadequacies, sin and their consequences.
The King has one more move and, if we let Him,
that transformation can begin!

God's love for us is His power.
He is able to drive a stake through the heart of
whatever demonic grip is on our lives.
Our passion for the possible is based in this:
"He who is in you is greater than he who is in the world!" [6]

As the Apostle Paul writes:
"If anyone *is* in Christ, *he is* a new creation;
old things have passed away; behold, all
things have become new." 7

The Living Bible translation is:
"When someone becomes a Christian, he
becomes a brand new person inside.
He is not the same anymore.
A new life has begun!"

God is able to change our so-called liabilities into opportunities.

I recently heard about a young man in Hawaii
who was in a terrible car accident
and lost his left arm.
He was deeply depressed. His father,
trying to encourage him, asked
"Can I do anything? Is there anything I can do for you?"

The boy said, "Yes. I would like to take judo lessons.
I understand you can do judo with one arm."

The father got his son a sensei, a teacher, to teach him judo.
After learning the basics of the art of judo,
the sensei concentrated on one move, just one move alone.
That one move, over and over and over again,
day after day, week after week.

After two-and-a-half months, the sensei said to the boy,
"You're entering a tournament."
The boy said, "You've got to be kidding.
I've only been taking judo for two-and-a-
half months. I only have one arm.
My left arm is gone and I'm going to be in a tournament."

They went to the tournament and the boy won the first round,
then the second and third rounds.
The boy couldn't believe it.
He kept on winning right up until the final round and he won!
On the way home he said to the sensei, "I don't
understand. How is this possible?
I've only been taking judo for two-and-a-half-months.

I really only know one move.
How could I have beaten the champion of the state?"

The sensei said, "You won for two reasons.
First, the one move you know is the most
effective move in all of judo.
The second reason is because the only defence against that move
is to grab your opponent's left arm - and you don't have a left arm!"

**God doesn't look at our inadequacies,
He looks at our possibilities!**

Our faith infuses our spirits with a passion for
the possible and, with that passion,
we are able to overcome whatever obstacle
life causes to come against us.

Are you facing a seemingly impossible problem?

The former President of the McDonnell Douglas Corporation,
during the early days of space exploration said,
"There is no such thing as an insoluble problem!
What appears to be an impossible problem is
merely a temporary setback to ingenuity."
He noted the unbelievable number of "unsolvable" problems

that was handled in the first three-man scientific
laboratory to be sent into outer space.
He was asked, "How did you solve so many complex problems?"

His answer contains universal principles we can all use:
No matter how big the problem is,
break it down until you get the smallest lump,
and solve it, and then solve another –
until you put the solved parts together like a jigsaw puzzle.
Success is a matter of not quitting and failure
is a matter of giving up too soon.

One of the most baffling questions waiting
to be responsibly answered
by psychological researchers today is
whether an all-consuming drive
can create talent where talent presumably does not exist.
There is mounting evidence that this may indeed be true.

John Stewart, the New York City Opera Company star,
was advised by "experts" that his voice just
"isn't the instrument of a professional singer".
He was advised to give up his desire to perform
and prepare instead to teach music.

No one today doubts that he has talent.
It appears that talent is the description given by an approving public
to a disciplined, determined, dedicated, and undefeatable dreamer
who is driven by an all-consuming desire to succeed.

Can a mentally challenged Mongoloid child have
the natural talent to become teachable?
Of course not!
Or so the experts have always agreed.

Yet amazing things are happening in the
mentally challenged section
of the public school in Mitchell, South Dakota.
There one sees twelve youngsters fired up
with an incredible desire to learn.

A teacher in that school had her whole class read whole sentences,
despite the predictions of other similar teachers in other schools!
She said, her eyes flashing with excitement,
"We haven't begun to discover how much
talent these youngsters have."

Dr. Irving Stone, an eminent psychologist
specializing in working with the severely
mentally challenged children
in Fairview State Hospital in Costa Mesa, California,
listened to the account of the school in South Dakota and enthused,
"It's so true.
We have just come to the conclusion that
as far as the learning ability
of these children is concerned our official policy
must change to - anything is possible!"

"We now know that we have been limiting these persons
by our own lack of belief in that vast unfathomed
potential lying dormant in their minds.
It now appears that OUR minds have been clouded
in imagining what they can accomplish
if they are properly motivated, inspired, and trained."

Be passionate about your unlimited possibilities!

Believe in the potential of God's unlimited
power to work to achieve your dreams.

We are always surrounded by too many "dream stealers"
who are so eager to tell us what we cannot do.
Don't listen to them!
Rather focus on what the Lord can accomplish in your life.
Focus is the key word.

Don't be distracted from your dream by
negative circumstances and criticism,
or the allure of seemingly better dreams!

Remember how God encouraged Joshua
as Joshua stood on the edge of his dream
of entering the Promised Land:

"No man shall *be able* to stand before you all the days of your life;
as I was with Moses, so I will be with you.
I will not leave you nor forsake you...
be strong and very courageous, that you may observe to do
according to all the law which Moses My servant commanded you;
<u>do not turn from it to the right hand or to the left</u>,
that you may prosper wherever you go.

This Book of the Law shall not depart from your mouth,
but you shall meditate in it day and night,
that you may observe to do according to all that is written in it.

For then you will make your way prosperous,
and then you will have good success.
Have I not commanded you?
Be strong and of good courage; do not be afraid, nor be dismayed,
for the LORD your God is with you wherever you go." [8]

Joshua's fellow spies, a generation before, had
allowed their dream to be stolen through fear.

God, therefore, had to remove any fear from Joshua's spirit
to be the required leader and He said to Joshua:
Don't be distracted from your goal!
Don't turn to the right or the left!
Focus!
God says the same words to us as we are distracted by negativism
and calls us to be passionate about our possibilities!

The German philosopher Nietzsche wrote
of the impact of negativism:
**"If you gaze too long into an abyss,
the abyss gazes also into you."**

If we allow criticism and the message of the
dream stealers to seep into our spirits
we will become infected by that "darkness" and lose our passion.

Focus!

Don't stare into the abyss of failure,
stare into the Word of God which says to us:
**"God has not given us a spirit of fear, but of power
and of love and of a sound mind."** [9]

I am always inspired to hear how so many
super successful men and women
suffered significant defeats before their final success.
They refused to gaze into that abyss of failure
and allow defeat to dominate their spirits.

Imagine how James Cash Penney felt when he lost $40 million
in the stock market crash of 1929.
To really understand his despair think of
the value of that $40 million
in today's financial terms.

Penney became deathly ill from the stress of his circumstances.
Seven million dollars in debt, he wrote:
"I was convinced I would never see another dawn.
I wrote farewell letters to my family.
Then I waited for the end - a failure at the age of 56!"

Although Penney felt he had no future, God had other plans.
At the Battle Creek Sanitarium in Michigan
where he was being treated for his illness,
Penney one day heard the hymn, "God will take care of you".
He decided to trust the Lord and he made a commitment to Christ.
Not only did he survive, he also lived into his nineties,
building a financial empire through his J C Penney stores.

**GOD DOESN'T LOOK AT
OUR INADEQUACIES;
HE LOOKS AT OUR POSSIBILITIES!**

"IF YOU GAZE TOO LONG
INTO AN ABYSS,
THE ABYSS GAZES ALSO INTO YOU."
(Nietzsche)

Each of us has wept over difficulties and
struggles we thought we couldn't survive.
But stand firm on your faith that God has other plans for your life,
regardless how your present circumstances appear.

If you are experiencing devastating difficulties today
or see disturbing troubles bearing down on you,
build your trust in the Lord and believe that
HE CAN MAKE A WAY WHERE THERE IS NO WAY!

<u>God will make a way where there is no way!</u>

Hold fast to the message of I Peter:
" 'God resists the proud, but gives grace to the humble.'
Therefore humble yourselves under the mighty hand of God,
that He may exalt you in due time,
casting all your care upon Him, for He cares for you." [10]

We have been brought up with the mentality
of handling our own problems
with the result that, when we encounter
problems beyond our capacity to handle,
we buckle under the pressure.

The person of faith does not abdicate personal responsibility but,
rather than functioning alone,
harnesses the unlimited power and creativity of God.
In full humility, they give their lives over to
God's direction and find true success.
It is this dependent relationship
that ensures success and powers through failures to victory.

The person of faith embraces Jeremiah's spirit of trusting God,
believing God will guide us into His future for us.
Therefore, we don't quit!

I was astounded to learn that one of the biggest gold
deposits ever excavated in the United States
was discovered just two inches beneath the spot
where a previous miner had given up?
There are many great blessings we will lose
if we give up and lose our passion for the possible.

Whenever you are tempted to give up, focus on the Living Lord.
Cling to Him with all your heart, soul, strength
and mind, regardless what happens.
Stand on His promise:

**"The LORD, He is the One who goes before you.
He will be with you,
He will not leave you nor forsake you;
do not fear nor be dismayed."** [11]

When God commanded the Children of
Israel to cross the Jordan River
and possess the land He had sworn to give them,
He told them about the difficulties they would face and

"A people great and tall, the descendants
of Anakim, whom you know,
and of whom you have heard it said,
'Who can stand before the descendants of Anak?'
Therefore understand today that the LORD
your God is He who goes before you
as a consuming fire.
He will destroy them and bring them down
before you; so you shall drive them out
and destroy them quickly, as the LORD has said to you." [12]

Whenever you are told:
"It can't be done! The problem is too big!
Those opposing you are too strong and have
too many powerful contacts!"
Remember that the Lord your God goes
before you and fights for you
in ways beyond your understanding.
As you stand filled with the passion for the
possible you will achieve the victory!

Always avoid the dream stealers.
Refuse to get involved in their arguments.
Focus on God!
Believe that before we have the problem, God has the solution!
Stand in the Biblical stream of faith that insists God goes before us
and knows what's in our future and He will
make sure that the right people
are in the right place at the right time to help us.
We fuel our passion for the possible through
our belief that God is in control
and that as we stay in faith He will make a
way where there seems to be no way.

God's got a million different ways in which He can make it happen!

The Apostle Paul was a man so possessed
by this passion that he could say:
"I can do all things through Christ who strengthens me." [13]

When you are confronted by your dream
stealers who say "You can't do it!"
remember what they are really saying is "I can't do it!"

Don't let anyone demean your abilities or your faith in God.
Look at these examples of people who were demeaned:

- Dismissed from drama school with a note that stated,
  "You're wasting your time - too shy to put your best foot forward." -
  Lucille Ball.

- Turned down by the Decca Recording Company, saying,
  "We don't like your sound and guitar music is on the way out." -
  The Beatles.

- Cut from the high school basketball team for being too short
  (5' 10"), he went home, locked himself in his room and cried. -
  Michael Jordan.

- A teacher told him he was too stupid to learn anything and he
  should go into a field where he might succeed by virtue of his
  pleasant personality - **Thomas Edison.**

- Fired from a newspaper because he lacked imagination and had
  no original ideas - **Walt Disney.**

- A young business student at Yale University submitted his
  business plan to his management professor, who responded:
  "This concept is interesting and well-formed, but in order to
  earn better than a 'C', the idea must be feasible."

That student, **Fred Smith**, went ahead
and started his company **FedEx.**
It turned out to be a very feasible business, with
more than $6 billion a year in revenues.

No matter the criticism of others,
God never gives up on the dreams He has planted inside each of us.

When we encounter storms of opposition,
begin to emulate the Eagle which can fly over
10,000 feet, high above the storm.
We all face disappointments, failed dreams, even tragedies,
but we don't have to be shackled by them.
Our past does not define our future!
We are the Easter people who proclaim
the resurrection of dead dreams
and a new beginning by the power of God!

Our past does not have to define our future!

Keep on with your passion for the possible.
Believe God has created you for a special destiny.
Be confident about yourself, for we are
children of the Most High God.
There is divine DNA in each one of us. Paul
encourages us with these words:

**"Being confident of this very thing,
that He who began a good work in you will complete it."** [14]

Another translation states:
"God will bring you to a flourishing finish!"

Despite your present, in faith speak victory into your future.
You may have been through heartache and pain.
But the depth of your past foretells the height of your future.
When a skyscraper is being constructed high into the sky,
the builders must first dig low
to give it a solid foundation.
Only then can the structure rise to its full height.

Your foundation is being formed. It may be taking a long time, but if you will stay in faith, God is preparing you.
Don't compromise your future!
You have too much to lose!

In the face of your adversity have the faith which believes:

**"That which does not kill me,
only makes me stronger"**
(Nietzsche)

CHAPTER 7

PASSION THROUGH PRAISE!

Corrie ten Boom was a middle-aged,
traditional Dutch Christian woman
when her whole family was sentenced to
the Nazi concentration camps
for hiding Jews during World War II.
She and her frail sister Betsie ended up in Ravensbruck,
a veritable hell on earth.

In the claustrophobic conditions of their barracks,
Corrie woke one morning being bitten by fleas.
As they lay on their straw-covered platforms,
struggling against the nausea that swept
over them from the reeking straw,
this seemed the final outrage and Corrie began
to complain bitterly to her sister,
saying "Betsie, how can we live in such a place?"

Betsie said, "Show us. Show us how."
It was said so matter of factly
that it took Corrie a while to realize her sister was praying.
"Corrie," Betsie said excitedly, "He's given us the answer!
Before we asked, as He always does!
In the Bible this morning. Read that part again!"

Corrie took the Bible they smuggled into the
barracks from its hidden place and,

turning to First Thessalonians, she read:
"Rejoice always, pray without ceasing, in everything give thanks;
for this is the will of God in Christ Jesus for you." [1]

"That's it, Corrie! That's His answer.
'Give thanks in all circumstances!' That's what we can do.
We can start right now to thank God for every
single thing about this new barracks."

Corrie stared at her, then around at the dark, foul-aired room.
"Such as?" she said.
"Such as being assigned here together."
Corrie bit her lip, but said, "Oh yes, thank you Lord Jesus."
"Such as what you're holding in your hands," said Betsie.
Corrie looked down at the Bible.
"Yes, thank you, dear Lord,
that there was no inspection when we entered here!
Thank you for all these women, here in this
room, who will meet you in these pages."

"Yes," said Betsie, "Thank you for the very crowding here.
Since we are packed so close, that many more will hear."
"Thank you," Betsie went on serenely, "for the fleas."

For Corrie this was simply too much.
"Betsie, there's no way even God can make me thankful for a flea."

"Give thanks in ALL circumstances," Betsie quoted.
"It doesn't say, 'in pleasant circumstances'.
Fleas are part of this place where God has put us."

And so, as they stood between piers of
bunks and gave thanks for fleas,

Corrie realized that it was the very fleas,
and their fear of contagion,
that kept the prison wardens from coming into the barracks,
allowing the women to have their Bible study!

Give thanks for the fleas!

When we are able to look at our personal circumstances
through the prism of Paul's injunction:
**"No matter what happens, always be thankful,
for this is God's will for you who belong to Christ Jesus"** [2]
we will have fully entered the door to passionate praise.

**"The will of God will never lead us,
where the grace of God cannot keep us."**

Truly understanding this fact gives us the assurance
that God is in full control of our lives and that,
when we yield everything to Him, He guides
and sustains us for His purpose.

Praise is the passionate desire to be close to the Lord,
filled with thanksgiving for all He has
done and is doing in our lives,
whether we understand it or not,
and living with the confident expectation that
He will work for our good in the future.

"In everything give thanks!"

This was the prophet Jeremiah's experience
as he found hope even in the midst of devastation.
Whenever we are tempted to think that
such "passion for praise" is naïve,

consider his circumstance.
His city was sacked, his home destroyed,
many of his family and friends were
brutally murdered and maimed.
Weeping beside the torn-down walls of his burned and ruined city,
Jeremiah wrote this woeful funeral psalm:

"O Lord, all peace and all prosperity have long since gone,
for you have taken them away. I have forgotten what enjoyment is.
All hope is gone; my strength has turned to water,
for the Lord has left me.
Oh, remember the bitterness and suffering you have dealt to me!
For I can never forget these awful years;
always my soul will live in utter shame." [3]

But then the prophet of God looked into
the past and this is what he said:

"Yet there is one ray of hope: his compassion never ends.
It is only the Lord's mercies that have
kept us from complete destruction.
Great is his faithfulness;
his loving-kindness begins afresh each day.
My soul claims the Lord as my inheritance;
therefore I will hope in him.
The Lord is wonderfully good to those who wait for him,
to those who seek for him.
It is good both to hope and wait quietly
for the salvation of the Lord." [4]

When devastation strikes unexpectedly and undeservedly,
we look into the past and remember the
goodness and guidance of God.
Then we are able to look into the future

and build up our hope as we persistently
and passionately praise God!
For the secular person this is both naïve and foolish,
but to the person who stands in faith this
praise has delivering power.

Recall the situation of Paul and Silas who,
after being severely beaten, were thrown into jail.
There is very little to compare this treatment
with in our so-called civilized world.
Our only comparison are images of torture.

Paul and Silas came to Philippi, where they
were accused of corrupting the city
and were stripped and beaten with whips until
the blood ran from their bare backs.
**"The jailer...put them into
the inner dungeon and clamped their feet into the stocks."** [5]

It takes only a little imagination
to understand the brutality and desperation of their condition!

They sat there in the dungeon with the
blood stiffened on their sore backs,
unable to stretch their aching legs.
Talk about physical pain!
But they did not believe God had deserted them,
being fully convinced He had called them to preach in Philippi.

Then the Scripture states:
**"At midnight Paul and Silas were praying and singing hymns
to God, and the prisoners were listening to them."** [6]

Then came their deliverance through an
earthquake that rocked the prison.

"Midnight" can well be a metaphor for our tragic circumstances
when we are tempted to complain and despair.
But there is no deliverance in that attitude,
however justified it may seem.

It is through focusing on God, giving Him "praise and thanks",
that we and our situations begin to change.

In World War II,
the most dangerous convoys were the ships
taking the northern route to Russia.
Out of the hellish experience of bitter cold
and air and submarine attacks
there came this affirmation of hope:
"To all things an end, to every night its dawn;
even to the longest night when dawn never comes,
there comes at last the dawn."

That's the indomitable courage of the human spirit.
Imagine that spirit reinforced by the Holy Spirit!

We have made prayer and praise so complex
that we come before God concerned about the
sentence structure of our prayers;
using the correct words of adoration and supplication,
it blocks out the intimacy the Lord seeks from us.
Some of the best prayers I've ever prayed
have started like this: "HELP!"

When you're in real trouble you don't have time to pray,
"Lord, if Thou wouldest, and shouldest,
and couldest, Thou mightest!"

Simply pray, "**HELP!**"
God understands that!

Do you need a miracle?
Start praising the Lord with thanksgiving and
He will open the windows of heaven.
In trouble, pray:
"Lord, I thank you for the trial I'm going through.
I don't understand it.
I know you're too wise to make a mistake
and too loving to be unkind.
I'm going through a Gethsemane.
My pillow is wet with the tears I am shedding
but I know that you know where I am going.

I thank you for the business crisis.
I will not become bitter. I will not become
angry. I will not become resentful.
Yet will I praise you, the Glory and Lifter of my head,
knowing that you are leading me right now
to the greatest business opportunity of my life.
I give you praise and glory, although I don't feel like it!
I glorify the Resurrected Son of God –
THE ANSWER IS ON THE WAY!"

When we start praying like that every
negative force against us vanishes,
miracles start happening, walls start
falling, and seas start dividing.

God will not fail us!
That's the basis of our praise!

When we are challenged by difficulties,
complaining comes so easily that we often
don't realize what we are doing.
But complaining is the very opposite of praise and trust.

A complaint has been defined as an accusation.

By complaining and grumbling we are actually accusing God
of mismanaging the details of our lives.
Praise, however, releases the power of God,
which our complaining blocks.
When the Israelites were delivered from Egypt,
they kept on complaining about so many things
that God caused that generation not to
enter into the Promised Land.

The root of the Israelites' complaining was unbelief.
Like them, unbelief is at the root of every one of our complaints.
We need to understand that "unbelief" is
a serious offence against God.
Jesus said, " 'The world's sin is unbelief in me.' " [7]
Unbelief, like all sin, is an act of rebellion against God.

Unbelief blocks God's blessings to us!

Can you accept and declare to yourself that God
has you exactly where he wants you?
Do you believe that God hasn't overlooked anything -
that He wasn't helpless to interfere back
when you made wrong choices?
We are always responsible for our choices
and the good or bad consequences of those choices.
But God's promise is that He makes all things,
including our own wrong choices and their consequences,

work for our good when we trust Him and
give Him full control of our lives.

Praise releases God's power into our lives!

Many Biblical stories illustrate this point but, perhaps,
none more powerfully so than the battle which
King Jehoshaphat of Judah faced.
His tiny kingdom was surrounded by the
powerful armies of his enemies.
The king knew that Judah didn't have a chance in its own might,
so he cried out to God:
**" 'We have no power against this great
multitude that is coming against us;
nor do we know what to do, but our eyes are upon You.' "** [8]

Likewise, we are not blind to the tough situations we face.
However, seeing them for what they are gives us greater cause
to praise and thank God for working in those
situations with perfect control and authority.
We are not pre-occupied with the negatives around us.
We see them, admit our helplessness to cope
with them in our own strength,
and then turn to God.

God said to Jehoshaphat:
**" 'Do not be afraid nor dismayed because of this great multitude,
for the battle is not yours, but God's.' "** [9]

That statement is our guiding faith principle
leading us to peace and victory!
We don't always have the ability to cope with
our challenging circumstances,
so obviously the battle isn't ours, but God's.

God says:
" 'You will not *need* to fight in this *battle*.
Position yourselves, stand still
and see the salvation of the LORD, who is with you.' " [10]

Now what did Jehoshaphat do while standing
still and waiting for God to act?

This is where the story becomes amazing.
The next morning he organized praise teams to go before the army:
" '…singing the song His Loving-Kindness Is Forever'
as they walked along praising and thanking the Lord!" [11]

This scene took place right in front of the amassed armies
ready to slaughter the army of Judah.
Their reaction must have been one of
absolute astonishment and ridicule!
It's in this kind of situation that our own understanding
is most likely to resist and try and formulate a "realistic" solution.

We might say:
"It's all well and good to praise the Lord when we're in a tough spot,
but let's not get ridiculous about this!
God helps those who help themselves.
The least we can do is go out there and
fight as valiantly as we know how.
Then we'll leave the rest to God."

But look what happened to Jehoshaphat and the people of Judah.

"Now when they began to sing and to praise,
the LORD set ambushes against the people…who had
come against Judah; and they were defeated.
For the people stood up against the inhabitants of

Mount Seir to utterly kill and destroy them.
And when they had made an end of the
inhabitants of Seir, they helped to destroy one another." [12]

When the enemy was destroyed
the people of Judah went and plundered all
the wealth they had left behind.

Too many of us are defeated by our circumstances
because we aren't ready to accept the fact that,
if we belong to God, the battle is God's and not ours.
Even when we realize our own powerlessness
to cope with our "enemies",
we are afraid to let go, and completely trust
ourselves to God's resources.
When seeking solutions to our "impossible problems",
men and women of faith state:

**"Trust God.
He's got a million ways to make it happen!"**

We allow our desire for understanding to overpower us
and take the wrong position in our lives.
We say, "I don't understand; therefore, I don't believe!"
But God's Word clearly states that the only way
out of our dilemmas is through faith.
We are called to believe God's promises
are true and, accepting them,
dare to trust in those promises,
even though we don't understand how they can come to pass.
The Biblical principle is this:

"Acceptance comes before understanding!"

The reason for this is simple.
Our human understanding is so limited
that we cannot possibly grasp the magnitude
and intricacy of God's plan for our lives.
Trusting Him with complete abandonment
is the key to rising to new levels of deliverance.

Recently, I read an article about Pastor David Oyedepo of Nigeria,
a man of deep personal faith and pastoral achievement.
He reminds us that one of the most grievous
sins mentioned in Scripture
was to **"murmur against God".** [13]

It was then that he discovered the power of praise.
He explained that prayer is wonderful, because prayer draws angels.
But God inhabits our praise!
He realized that if he wanted God to show up in his situation,
he could draw His presence through praise.
He believes you can praise your way out of any situation.
When businessmen in his church tell him they are losing money,
his advice is always the same.
'If you have ten minutes to pray, be sure that
seven of them are spent in praise.'

Oyedepo says that in the secular world you only say thank you
to someone who has done something for you worthy of thanks.
But in the Kingdom of God, **until** you say thank you to God,
nothing gets done.

Since he stumbled on that truth,
he spends 90% of his time in God's presence in thanksgiving.
Thanksgiving is the spiritual yeast that brings
multiplication wherever it is found.
When you praise God you allow Him to enforce what is written,
contrary to what is happening in your life.

Our praise-filled faith focuses, not on the
problem, but on the solution.
We search the Word for God's answer to our problem,
meditate on it,
and that 'word' supernaturally expands our capacity for faith,
renewing our minds to think God's thoughts.

" 'For My thoughts are not your thoughts,
Nor are your ways My ways,' says the LORD.
'For as the heavens are higher than the earth,
So are My ways higher than your ways,
And My thoughts than your thoughts...
My word shall not return to Me void,
But it shall accomplish what I please,
And it shall prosper *in the thing* for which I sent it.' " [14]

God has answers to our problems far beyond our comprehension.
A businessman went to one of the Arab emirates
to do some work for the United States.
Once he had concluded his business,
the head of the royal family said they
would like to give him a present.
The man replied that he didn't need a gift.

But the member of the family insisted, saying it
was a tradition which they must follow.
So, over the protests of the businessman, he
asked what the man would like.
Not wanting to give offence,
the businessman finally said that he would like a "golf club".

He returned to the United States and, after about three weeks,
there was a knock on his door from a man who said,
"Sir, I'd like you to follow me and I will take you to your golf club."

He took the man over to an 18-hole golf club
with a putting green, club house – all was his.

Look at the situation.
Both the businessman and the member of the
royal family were saying the same thing,
but their thoughts were completely different.

Just two words: "Golf club!"
One man was thinking about a 'nine iron';
the other was thinking about some real estate.

What is God thinking about in the Bible?
Have we taken some things and brought them
down to the level of a 'nine iron',
while God is saying "Your thoughts are not my thoughts!"
He is thinking far beyond our comprehension and,
though we may both say the same words,
our thoughts are totally different.

Praise releases the breadth of God's thoughts into our lives!

This is why we should pay such close attention to Jesus' words,
" 'Out of the abundance of the heart the mouth speaks.' " [15]

Our 'words' reflect who we are and 'where' we are going.
We speak about that which is uppermost in
our minds, and our real desires.
We 'speak' our state of mind,
and we 'speak' our goals and dreams for our lives.
Too many of us have forgotten, if we ever knew this truth,
that we must carefully monitor our words,
for those words are going to govern our
lives and determine our destiny.

"Keep your heart with all diligence,
For out of it spring the issues of life." [16]

We must carefully watch what we take into our hearts,
through our 'eyes', our 'ears', and through our 'spoken words'.
These are the three gateways to the heart
which determine our present and future condition and our praise!
Make sure the only information going into
our hearts is pure and positive
and based on the Word of God.
Only then will we be truly able to speak words of praise!

Jesus lashed the religious leaders of his
day, denouncing them, saying:

" 'Brood of vipers!
How can you, being evil, speak good things?
For out of the abundance of the heart the mouth speaks.
A good man out of the good treasure of his
heart brings forth good things,
and an evil man out of the evil treasure
brings forth evil things.' " [17]

When our hearts and words line up together in praise to God
we begin to grow and flourish in every area of our lives.
It is therefore crucial to monitor that heart-mouth combination,
making sure that our hearts are only filled
with and nurtured by positive,
creative thoughts, words, and images.
Then what we speak will be consistent with
God's spirit and intention for us.

This does not mean we ignore the negative,
destructive things around us.

Rather, it means we do not exalt them over the spirit of God.
We look at our lives and the world, not
through rosy coloured glasses,
but with the eyes of creative, transforming faith.
We strive to live and speak the words of praise and faith in God,
if we want our lives to reflect that faith and
power which determines our destiny.

Negativism only breeds more negativism!

We must guard our hearts and mouths continually
to ensure they only speak praise!

The Nazi propagandist, Goebbels, maintained
the power of words when he stated:
"It doesn't matter how big the lie - if it is told
often enough it will be believed."

"Death and life are in the power of the tongue." [18]

There is a story from the Middle Ages of
a man who went to see a monk.
He had been telling lies about someone.
What should he do?
The monk told him to go and put a feather
on every doorstep in the community.
The man quickly went away and did as he was instructed.

Then he came back to the monk and asked what he should do next.
Now, the monk told him to go back into the
community and pick up all the feathers.
The man said that would be impossible as, by now,
the wind would have blown them all away.
The monk told the man that is what had
happened with his words (lies).

Someone wrote these words:
"My name is gossip.
I have no respect for justice.
I maim without caring.
I break hearts and ruin lives.
I'm cunning, malicious,
and gather strength with age.
The more I'm greeted the more I'm believed.
I flourish in every level of society.
My victims are helpless.
They cannot protect themselves against me
because I have no face.
To track me down is impossible.
The harder you try, the more elusive I become.
I am nobody's friend.
Once I tarnish a reputation
it is never the same.
I topple governments, wreck marriages, ruin careers,
cause sleepless nights and heartache.
I spawn suspicion and generate grief.
I make innocent people cry on their pillows,
and even my name hisses - GOSSIP!"

One writer states:
"Gossip is hearing something you like about someone you don't!
It's the speedy transmission of near factual information.
It isn't the thing that goes in one ear and out the other that hurts,
as much as the thing that goes in one ear, gets all mixed up,
and then slips out the mouth..."

Today, Gossip is the fuel that drives many TV
talk shows, newspapers and magazines.
It's amazing how a gossip can give you all the
details without knowing any of the facts.

Gossip seems to travel fastest over grapevines that are slightly sour.
We talk about hearing 'juicy gossip'.

And when people say, 'I probably shouldn't tell you this!'
why don't we reply, 'Well, you better not.'
Instead, we reply, 'Oh, go on! What is it?' "

The Spirit of the Lord cannot live in such
destructive behaviour. Scripture states:

"Let us love one another, for love is of God;
and everyone who loves is born of God and knows God.
He who does not love does not know God,
for God is love…
If we love one another, God abides in us,
and His love has been perfected in us.
By this we know that we abide in Him, and He in us,
because He has given us of His Spirit.
And we have known and believed the love that God has for us.
God is love, and He who abides in love
abides in God, and God in him." [19]

This spirit empowers our passion for praise.
Realizing what God has done for us in Christ
in His life, death and resurrection,
and the continuing work of the Spirit,
our spirits look to God with thanksgiving and praise,
knowing that He accepts us as we are, without condemnation,
transforming us into the people we were created to be.
If we are to be empowered to praise with real passion
there is no room for strife, anger or unforgiveness.

A life of passionate praise!

"WHEN YOU PRAISE GOD,
YOU ALLOW HIM TO ENFORCE
WHAT IS WRITTEN,
CONTRARY TO WHAT IS
HAPPENING IN YOUR LIFE."

CHAPTER 8

PASSION FOR PURPOSE!

A university professor tells how there is usually one event
he can count on happening every May.
Some students will come to him and say they are
not coming back for the next semester.
When asked the reason, the students will
invariably reply in some form,
"I need time to find myself!"

The students then can become quite intense
and talk about the need to peel away
the layers of identity and expectation
superimposed on them by their parents,
their society, their peers, the church, or whatever other influence.

The professor challenges them asking,
"What happens if you peel away all these layers
and then find that there's nothing there?"
He tells how Jesus said,
**"Whoever desires to save his life will lose it,
but whoever loses his life for My sake
and the gospel's will save it."** [1]

The professor's central point is this:
the self is not waiting to be discovered through introspection,
but rather waiting to be created through commitment.
Commitments define us.
Commitments give each of us our identity.

If we have no commitments we are, as the poet T.S. Elliot says,
"The hollow men, the straw men, blown to and fro by the wind." [2]

One sociologist states:
Ours is the generation of the uncommitted
and it is our commitments that make us fully
human and of real value in our world.
We are more than the result of the moulding forces of our past.
We are defined by what we choose to become.
What makes us more than animals
is that we are moulded more by the future than the past.

Our commitments define us!

Our world is desperate for men and women
who are completely committed
to their highest ideals.
Dr. Margaret Mead writes:
**"Never doubt that a small group of
thoughtful, committed citizens
can change the world.
Indeed, it is the only thing that ever has."**

God is waiting to take us,
mould us through the tests we encounter,
and enable us to become the people He needs
us to be for His purpose in the world.

A master contractor said to a previously
highly-ambitious young priest
who had been through fiery tests,
"Once I thought you were ambitious.
I see now that the fire of the Holy Spirit has
burned that ambition right down to cinders.

But did you know that cinder blocks make
the best building material?
Stuff that's passed through the fire to ash
can't be burned by anything else.
Master contractors know that."

It is as we commit ourselves with passion
to the highest ideals we know,
that we are able to achieve our greatest fulfillment.
We transcend the superficiality of self-centeredness
and become committed to the welfare of
the whole family of our world.

**"We are as young as our dreams,
and as old as our cynicism."**

Therefore, dream large dreams with passion!

I was privileged to hear world-renowned
psychiatrist Dr. Viktor Frankl
speak on the subject: "Is the New Generation Mad?"
The subject had been given him by the head of the student body
of a large American university.

Due to a severe thunderstorm the plane was diverted
and he had to land at another airport and
take a taxi for the rest of the journey.
The taxi driver asked him what he was doing
at the university in such weather.
Frankl replied, "I have to deliver a lecture tonight."
"What are you speaking on?" asked the taxi driver.
"IS THE NEW GENERATION MAD?"

The taxi driver laughed and Frankl said,
"Don't laugh but accept this proposition.
I take over your car and you take over my lecture."

"I couldn't do that," said the taxi driver.
"Why not?" asked Frankl.
"After all you, more than I, have the finger on the pulse of the time.
You know your young people better than I.
I came from Vienna just yesterday.
Do you think that the New Generation is mad?"

Like a pistol shot the taxi driver replied,
"Of course they are!
They kill themselves!
They kill each other!
And they take dope!"

That taxi driver, said Frankl, "without knowing,
had pointed out what I would like to call
the mass neurotic triad:
the three main aspects of the modern mass neurosis:
people, due to a feeling of meaninglessness,
are inclined to kill themselves - DEPRESSION, up to suicide.
Second, they kill each other - AGGRESSION.
Third, they take dope - ADDICTION."

In this fragmented, disoriented and increasingly empty society
Dr. Frankl developed what he calls "LOGOTHERAPY" –
healing through meaning.
He insists categorically that "man's primary
concern is the will to meaning."

The mass neurosis of today is the feeling of meaninglessness!

Patients no longer complain of inferiority and sexual frustration
as they did in the age of Adler and Freud.
Today they come to see psychiatrists because of feelings of futility.

Albert Camus, the French philosopher, once said,
"There is but one truly serious problem,
and that is…judging whether life is or is not worth living."

I was reminded of this when I was shown a report
in which a high school teacher invited his students
to present him with any question they wished,
and they might do so anonymously.
The questions ranged from drug addiction
to sexuality to life on other planets.
But the one most frequent question was about suicide.

Among college students suicide is second only to traffic accidents
as the most frequent cause of death.
But when one factors in "suicide attempts",
the statistics become fifteen times more frequent!

This happens in the midst of affluent societies and welfare states.
Economic status is not the issue.
The truth is that as the struggle for survival has subsided,
the question has emerged: "Survival for what?"

At Harvard University among graduates who
went on to lead quite successful,
seemingly happy lives, a huge percentage
complained of a deep sense of futility,
asking themselves what all their success had been for.
Doesn't this suggest that what is so often called a "mid-life crisis"
is actually a "crisis of meaning"?

With all the vast technological advances,
unheard of in previous generations,
men and women still yearn for inner meaning.

The German philosopher Nietzsche stated:
**"He who has a WHY to live for,
can bear with almost any HOW."**

In our computerized society it's easy to lose a
sense of meaning, of value, of identity.

There's a parallel for us in this experience of a
prisoner in a Nazi concentration camp.
He writes, "It's very difficult for an outsider
to grasp how very little value
was placed on human life in the camps.

The camp inmate was hardened, but possibly
became more conscious of this complete
disregard of human existence when a convoy
of sick men was organized.
The emaciated bodies of the sick were thrown on two-wheeled carts
which were dragged by prisoners for many miles,
often through snow storms to the next camp.

If one of the sick men had died before the cart left,
he was thrown on anyway –
the list had to be correct!
The list was the only thing that mattered.
A man counted only because he had a prison number.
One literally became a number, dead or
alive - that was unimportant;
the life of a 'number' was completely irrelevant."

In our world with its billions of people it's
quite easy to feel "just a number",
but in the sight of God that's a totally different reality.
The intimate knowledge of our Creator
of us is stated in Scripture as
"the very hairs of your heads are all numbered." [3]
God says:
" 'I knew you before you were formed
within your mother's womb.' " [4]

There's a whole different scenario of meaning here.
God created each of us with a distinct purpose
and strives to open our understanding to that truth.

A farmer's son had been out playing one day
and came home with a large, odd-looking egg.
The boy proudly showed it to his father
and asked if he could keep it.
The father didn't know exactly what to do with it,
so he went out to the barn and placed it under
a mother goose who was nesting.

A few days later the father and son were leaving the house
when they saw the mother goose come parading across the barnyard
followed by six beautiful baby geese.
It was a comical sight because the tiny new born creatures
were trying frantically to keep up with their mother.

The boy and his father smiled and started to turn around,
but then something caught their eye.
One of the little geese was trailing behind the rest.
His beak was not flat, it was pointed and twisted.
He could hardly walk because he had claws
instead of delicate webbed feet.

Instead of having lovely white plumes, he was an ugly brown color.
And to top it off, he made a terrible squawking sound!
He was some kind of freaky bird - so ugly and disfigured!

Then one day, a giant eagle flew across the
barnyard. He swept lower and lower
until the strange little awkward bird on the ground
lifted his head and pointed his crooked beak
into the sky to see what it was.

The misfit creature then stretched his wings out
and began to hobble across the yard.
He flapped his wings harder and harder
until the wind picked him up and carried him higher and higher.
He began to soar through the clouds.
He discovered what he was.
He was born an eagle, and he was trying to live like a goose!

We were born to soar!
We are children of God!
The tragedy is too many of us have never discovered our
divine heritage and so we live as little more than animals!

The story is told of a man who loved greyhound dogs.
He would go to the racetracks where they raced.
He would rescue them and bring them home.
A neighbour said, "I went to see my friend.
And there was this greyhound dog in the middle of the floor
wrestling with the children, having a great time.
They were kissing each other and rolling with each other."

The neighbour said, "I looked at that dog and said,
'Hey dog, why aren't you racing anymore? Are you too old?'
And the dog said, 'Oh, no... I'm still young.'

'Well why aren't you racing anymore? Weren't you winning races?'
'Oh, no,' said the dog, 'I was winning races right up until I quit.'
'Then why did you quit?'
And the dog said, 'Because one of these
days you'll realize what I realized.
I realized that the rabbit I was chasing wasn't real.' "

How many of us are chasing rabbits that aren't real?

This is where Jesus comes and lays bare His
optimal plan for our passionate pursuit.
He said, " **'Seek first the kingdom of God and His righteousness,
and all these things shall be added to you.' " ** [5]
(Matthew 6:33, NKJV)

This is the purpose that commands our fullest passion!

Seek God and His purpose FIRST!

Blaise Pascal went into a dark room one day and
sat down at seven o'clock that night.
He was determined not to get up until the
Spirit of God came rushing into his life.
He waited, and waited and waited, and the
next day he wrote in his diary:
"Ten thirty, pm, fire, fire, fire, joy, joy, joy." [6]

Not the God of the philosophers, nor the
God of the mathematicians,
nor the God of the theologians,
but the God that was alive in Abraham, Moses, and Jacob.

**Joy, joy, joy.
Fire, fire, fire.
Isn't that what you want?**

It becomes ours as we allow the Living Lord to come into our lives,
our control centers, transforming us to reveal
our specific passionate purpose!

Of course there are challenges that come to us all,
but they are used by God to shape and mould
us into the people he created us to be.
Every counselor has been asked the question: "Why? Why?
Why do these tough times happen to me?"

Testing the foundations!

In February 2011, a 6.3 earthquake devastated Christchurch,
the Garden City of New Zealand.
In September 2010 there was a larger earthquake some miles away,
of which this 6.3 quake is supposedly an "aftershock".
That first quake shook the foundations of buildings;
now they were leveled by this new catastrophe.

This natural disaster is an illustration of
what happens within our lives.
Tough times may be used by God to not
only develop our spiritual muscles,
but also to expose particular weaknesses.
Any weakness, however well hidden,
is like a crack in the foundation of a building.
Sooner or later, that crack under stress, will
cause the entire building to collapse.
The cracks we are aware of, we can do something about,
but we need the help of God to discern those "hidden weaknesses".

Our disobedience to God's leading is one such crack.
Too often we rely on ourselves, or follow the advice of others,
rather than obeying God's voice.

Self-reliance and self-assurance are good if they include God,
otherwise they are serious cracks that can
lead to personal collapse under crisis.

If God allows us to come under the pressure of circumstances
that reveal such self-sufficient tendencies, we
should give Him thanks for such exposure,
and harness His transforming power for further growth.

A young man in officer's training found
himself in such a circumstance.
He told his minister, "I need help, or I'll go out of my mind."
He had always been sure he could face
every circumstance with success.
His self-assurance bordered on arrogance.
But in the Officer's Candidate School,
he found himself unable to function as before
and his self-image was shattered.

The rigorous training is designed not only to
teach candidates their duties as officers,
but also to expose any weaknesses that might
endanger the lives of their men when in combat.
Stress is deliberately put on the candidates
to test what "stuff" they are made of
and see if they are going to crack under pressure.

The instructors sensed an inner insecurity under the
self-sufficient demeanor of this young man
and so they applied pressure from early morning
to late at night to challenge his self-esteem.

This candidate's confidence diminished rapidly.
Humiliated and helpless, he was at his wit's end,

ready to desert the army and leave the country, if
necessary, to get away from his "persecutors".

As he talked with his pastor, he confessed he
had never really believed in God,
and the Bible never made much sense to him.
But if there was a God who could help him, he wanted to believe.

The pastor shared that God had a perfect
plan for this young man's life
and that these trials were part of that plan,
designed to bring him into a closer relationship with God.
The candidate's face was drawn and he shook his head, saying:
"I'm at the end of my rope,
and now you're telling me that God placed me in this predicament?"

The pastor shared Paul's experience in his ministry:
"I think you ought to know… about the hard
time we went through in Asia.
We were really crushed and overwhelmed,
and feared we would never live through it.
We felt we were doomed to die and saw
how powerless we were to help
ourselves; but that was good,
for then we put everything into the hands of God,
who alone could save us." [7]

As the pastor prayed with the young man a new
understanding of God's love and concern
for every detail of his life, came to him.

A change began to take place.
He said, "God really did bring me to Officer's
Candidate School, didn't he?

He knew this is where I'd find the answer.
I feel like a new person."

Indeed he was.
He began a deep relationship with Christ
and went on to complete his training with excellent standing.
The crisis point in his life had revealed a
serious crack in his foundation.
When he could acknowledge and thank God
for His hand in the circumstance,
the crack was healed, and a new self-confidence developed.

One writer states:
"Circumstances that rip out the walls of our own self-sufficiency
are God's blessings in disguise.

We can thank God for them
and praise Him for every blow that removes more of the illusion
that we have the ability to handle our own
situations in our own strength.
We'll also discover that the more difficult the circumstance,
the more we will realize that the real strength and power
is Christ dwelling and growing in us."

The Apostle Paul discovered this truth when he
wrestled with his "thorn in the flesh".
He asked God three times to take it away, but God refused saying,
"My strength is made perfect in weakness." [8]
Paul's response was:
"Now I am glad to boast about how weak I am;
I am glad to be a living demonstration of God's power,
instead of showing off my own power and abilities.
For when I am weak, then I am strong -
the less I have, the more I depend on God." [9]

God wants us strong to complete His purpose for us,
so He will allow us to be thoroughly tested
to ensure that our entire foundation and structure is solid
through our complete dependence on Him.

Many of us draw strength from that great verse in Isaiah:
"Those who wait on the LORD shall renew their strength;
They shall mount up with wings like eagles,
They shall run and not be weary,
They shall walk and not faint." [10]

A counselor states:
"We all know what it means to be burned
out, whether professionally,
creatively, or productively.
Marriages burn out.
Individuals lose their enthusiasm for life.
The problem with burnouts is that they
inevitably lead to crash landings.

"God's given us the solution to burnouts - prayer.

When times are the toughest and it seems
as if you are as low as you can go,
you are in danger of a burnout.
It's precisely at those times you need God because
when you are in touch with God,
you are immune to burnout.
"You can be immune to 'burnouts', not 'brownouts'.
A brownout is a temporary power failure.

You may feel down in a brownout, but you
don't quit as you would in a burnout.
It's important to know the difference.

"In a 'brownout' the power will come back on.
To keep a 'brownout' from becoming a 'burnout'
you must remain in touch with God - that's what prayer is.

But remember, keeping in touch with God
won't eliminate your problems,
it will only help you manage them..."
With God inside you the power will come back on
and enable you to complete your purpose.

Whatever our circumstance, God is seeking
to strengthen our foundation
through deepening our relationship and communication with Him.

The ability to wait, to listen, to receive, and to obey,
is crucial in this effective communication.
We don't do all the talking,
without giving God a chance to answer and
our listening for that answer.

This pastor puts it well,
"For Jesus prayer was not to change God's mind, but to receive it...
What a difference this makes to our praying!
It is no longer an effort to get God's attention,
but attentive listening to what He has to say
about some need which is in our minds.
Once we understand that He is ready to give,
then we can pray with holy boldness."

If this is true, then it is not so much that God answers prayer,
as it is that His answer or direction is already awaiting our prayer.

Mahatma Ghandi,
upon arriving in England to seek a solution to India's problems,
said: "I'm doing this because a voice within me speaks."

Ghandi didn't mean a voice you could hear externally...
"Something" within spoke to him,
unmistakably, recognizably, positively;
and when it spoke, Ghandi followed the directions he received.

He knew that this "voice within" could
be depended on for guidance;
that when he properly prepared his mind to "hear" that voice,
he could await, with expectation and confidence, a definite message.

Ghandi didn't try to force this "voice" to
speak to him at certain times,
or to influence what it might say through wishful thinking.
But he always prepared his mind to listen
and then receive the message.

How to receive God's best!

Have you ever wondered how some people seem to receive so
much of God's blessings in their lives, while others do not?
I wondered whether some were specially gifted
by the talents with which they were born;
whether they had been destined for special functions by God.
But then I realized that the answer really was quite simple.
The extent to which we receive God's best
is determined ONLY by our capacity to receive!

Those whose lives are open to faith in the mighty acts of God,
who trust in His goodness and guidance, who
depend on Him for their strength,
are the ones whose lives are so obviously and
powerfully enriched by His blessing.
They know this trust intimately:
" 'Not by might nor by power, but by My Spirit,'
Says the LORD of hosts." [11]

It's against this background that we look at
those debilitating and destructive
forces in our lives:
not so much circumstances, as words!

Many of us were brought up in a time when this adage was recited:
"Sticks and stones can break your bones,
But words can never hurt you."
We now know this is foolishness!
Malicious and degrading words can destroy
our self-image and warp our destiny.
Most of us can recall all too well those
destructive words spoken over us.

I recall a friend telling me how he was travelling
with his parents to New York City
when he was eleven years old.
Because of some disagreement with his
father in Grand Central Station,
with hundreds of people watching, the father
slapped the boy across the face,
knocking off and breaking the boy's glasses,
loudly calling him, "A useless, ignorant fool!"
This was not an isolated incident,
but part of the process which moulded the negative self-image
against which this man had to contend all his life.

As a counselor, I hear many outrageous and bizarre incidents.
One such concerned a respected, church going family.
On the outside all seemed fine, but inside
was a totally different story.
The father and husband was a tyrant to all his family.
He kept a chair in the basement with a noose hanging above it,

symbolizing what the ultimate punishment
would be for misbehavior.
His violent and emotionally demeaning behaviour
reinforced the seriousness of that symbol.

Beware the words and images that impact your life!

No matter where we come from,
our past does not define our future!

Our future is determined by our faith in,
and our focus on, the Lord.

We are called to speak words of vibrant faith
and promise into our lives knowing that
"death and life are in the power of the tongue." [12]

We speak words of blessing into our own lives,
and the lives of our children,
cultivating the soil of our hearts to receive
the seed of God's purpose.

We fill our hearts with God's Word of Promise
thereby ensuring the soil we cultivate and the words we speak
will conform to God's will for us.

So we affirm our status of blessing as God's sons and daughters!
We hear and repeat again and again the
words of the prophet Balaam:
" 'How shall I curse whom God has not cursed...?
He has blessed, and I cannot reverse it.' " [13]

Do not let what someone has said about you,
or how someone raised you,

set negative limits on your life!
Realize that before anyone can put a 'curse' on you,
God put a Blessing,
and His Blessing always over-rides the curse!

When you really understand that you have been
blessed by the Creator of the Universe,
then no matter what comes against you, it will not affect you.
When someone talks negatively about you and
strikes to put you down, shake it off!
God is fighting your battles and He is your vindicator.

When someone tries to tear you down and weaken your future,
stay in faith,
for they don't know that what God has blessed no one can curse!
They meant it to harm you,
but God will cause it to backfire
and you will come out better than before!

When you understand who you are and
what God has already done then,
no matter what someone else did, or how unfair it was;
no matter how you were raised,
you won't get bitter living with a chip on your shoulder.

Rather, you will realize that nothing can stop you
from fulfilling your God given destiny!
You may have had dysfunctional parents
that put you at a disadvantage,
but **understand you didn't come FROM your mother,
you came THROUGH your mother.
YOU CAME FROM ALMIGHTY GOD!**
God used our mothers to get us here, but we came from God.

That means your destiny, your assignment, your purpose
cannot be ruined by who you came THROUGH –
you came FROM Almighty God.

I heard of a woman who was one of the so-called "cocaine babies".
Her mother had all kinds of addictions
and when this woman was born,
she was addicted as well as a baby.

Her mother left her at an early age and
now she is struggling with other
addictions and with her sense of identity and self-worth.
She was told this same principle I am sharing with you.
You came THROUGH your mother; love
her, respect her and pray for her,
but you didn't come FROM her.
You came from Almighty God and He has
already planned a great life for you.
You may have gotten off to a rough start,
but it's not how you start that matters, but how you finish.
It's been stated so powerfully:
Don't let your heredity stop your destiny!
Don't let how somebody treated you, or what they didn't do,
keep you from pressing forward and keeping
you from all that God created you to be.

Believe that "God put a Blessing on me before
anyone else could put a curse,
and I'm not going to let my heredity stop my destiny."
God knew who your parents would be.
Before you were ever a thought in their minds,
God had already planned out your life.

There is a powerful verse in Psalm 139 stating that God knew us,
even when we were an unformed substance.
He looked at that 'substance' and said:
this is My purpose for that person;
this is where they will live;
this is who their parents will be;
this is their assignment.
He then breathed His life into that 'substance'
and sent you THROUGH your mother,
and THROUGH your father.
They may have had issues but that doesn't have to stop you.
The Creator of the universe breathed His purpose into you.
The challenge for you is this: You are a person of destiny.
Have this realization deep down in your spirit.
You are not an accident.
You have been hand-picked by Almighty God
to be here at this time in history.

Sometimes we hear parents say:
We weren't expecting this child. They were a surprise.
They were an accident.
Not so!
You may have been a surprise to THEM,
But you were not a surprise to Almighty God!

No child can be born without God breathing His life into them.

You may think:
I was unwanted.
I was an unplanned pregnancy.
My mother and father weren't married.
But know this:
You wouldn't be here if God didn't give life to your seed!
In God's eyes there's no such thing as "illegitimate".

You didn't just show up unannounced, unwanted.
God had already planned out your days long
before you ever entered this world.

That's what God said to Jeremiah the Old Testament prophet:
**" 'Before I formed you in the womb I knew you…
I ordained you a prophet to the nations.' "** [14]

Notice Jeremiah had an assignment from
God before he was even born!

This fact has tremendous meaning for each one of us.
That means my past did not start with my
parents; or with my inherited DNA,
it started with my God!

Our parents may not have given us their blessing,
but the good news is that God gave us His Blessing FIRST!
The very fact that we woke up with an ability to breathe today
should be a reminder that we have been called,
chosen, anointed and set apart.
We are people of destiny!
Get rid of that "mistake", negative mentality;
realize that you have God's approval and
that's all that really matters.

When Israel Houghton's mother was first pregnant with him
she was a teenager growing up in Iowa, United States.
She was white and the father was black.
They weren't married.
This was back in the 1970's.
Her parents told her: "You are not going to keep this child.
It's a mistake.
You're going to ruin your life and the baby's life."

They gave her an ultimatum:
Either abort this baby or you're not welcome in our home!

Sadly, sometimes when our children need us
the most we help them the least.
That young girl made the decision to keep the baby.
She moved to California all by herself.
At 17 years of age she was on a street corner
when somebody talked with her
about finding peace with God.
That day, right then and there, she gave her life to Christ.

That person gave her a Bible and when she got home the first word
she saw was "Israel".
She thought: that's what I am going to name my baby!

Today we know that Israel was not a mistake.
He was not an accident.
He is one of the great worship leaders and song writers of our time.
He has written songs that are sung all over the world,
won Grammy Awards and all kinds of other accolades.
Israel could have sat around, with some
chip on his shoulder, thinking:
Why didn't I have a normal upbringing?
Why wasn't my father around?
Why do these kids make fun of me at school
because I'm half white and half black?

No, deep down in Israel Houghton's soul he
knew that he was a person of destiny.
He had a purpose to fulfill.
He says:
"Yes, I came THROUGH my mother and I love her,
but I came FROM Almighty God.

I know He has an assignment for me."
Israel didn't let his heredity stop his destiny!

You may believe you have a reason for the chip on your shoulder,
But you don't have a 'right'.
Almighty God breathed His life into you
and gave you an assignment.
You are not just here taking up space.
You are supposed to be pursuing your dreams
and making a difference in the world.
You've got to dig your heels in and say:
"I'm not settling where I am.
Life may have been unfair, but I know I am a person of destiny.
I realize that before anyone could put a curse on my life,
God put His Blessing on me!
So, I am going to rise up and become
everything He's anointed me to be!"

Get rid of the excuses for failure and rise up in faith and with
a holy determination press forward and you will see
God's plan for your life begin to unfold.
God will open up doors that no one can shut.
He will take what was meant for your harm
and use it to your advantage.

Remember this when you are tempted to despair:
the enemy doesn't fight you for where you are.
He fights you for where you are going.

He doesn't fight you for the present;
he fights you because he knows what is in your future!

The enemy would have loved to talk Israel's
mother into aborting him.

Why did the enemy fight her so hard?
He knew where Israel was going.
He knew her baby was going to do something great!

The enemy is fighting you now with that spirit of negativism
because he knows you are going to do damage to his kingdom
and that you are going to advance God's kingdom.

There will always be people who want to
keep you from rising higher,
talking behind your back, not inviting you to the right meetings,
not giving you the credit you deserve.
It's easy to get frustrated and want to fight back.
But I have learned the lesson that if you leave things to God,
and stay on the high road, that God will fight your battles for you.
It may look like they're getting the best of you,
keeping you from being promoted,
but don't get discouraged.
Your time is coming.
God always has the final say.
Others may keep you down temporarily but,
Like Balaam said: they are powerless to curse
those whom God has blessed!

In the face of negative circumstances:
<u>**SUCK IT UP!**</u>
God knows how to vindicate you!

Affirm with King David:
"Let them curse, but You bless." [15]

Some of you may have had to struggle
against a host of negative attacks;
you may be so worn down that you're not expecting God's blessings,

but get this truth inside you and hold fast to it:
"I may be discouraged now,
but I know the blessing that God has put on my life
will always override the damage others do to me!"

Don't ever say the Lord doesn't want to bless you!
He wants to bless you, but you've got to
be obedient to His calling.
Wait on the Lord and let God do for you
what only God knows how to do,
as He leads you into His perfect plan for your life!

When we feel alone, affirm His promise:
" 'I am with you always, even to the end of the age.' " [16]

When we feel defeated by circumstances, stand on His promise:
" 'Stand still, and see the salvation of the LORD...
For the Egyptians whom you see today, you
shall see again no more forever.' " [17]

What better example do we have than Job?
Regarding Job, God said:
" 'He is the finest man in all the earth –
a good man who fears God and will have
nothing to do with evil.' " [18]

When repeated calamities struck his life,
grinding him down into the very dust,
Job refused to curse God for his troubles, instead affirming:
" 'Though He slay me, yet will I trust Him.' " [19]

When you are discouraged, affirm with the Apostle Paul:
"Being confident of this very thing,
that He who has begun a good work in you will complete it." [20]

To those who think their purpose has bypassed
them as they focus on their inadequacies,
the call to reject their "loser image" is trumpeted
in this illustration of conception.

As one speaker said:
You were once a sperm. Not only were you once a sperm,
but you were once one of more than five million sperm in a group.
And you lined up at the starting line,
and at the end of a long, long tunnel, there was one egg.

And there was a race and you won!
The odds were five million to one and you came through!
Don't ever call yourself a loser!
You make the Olympics look like nothing!
Five million to one and you won!
You're a winner!

Receive your blessing!

As the son of a British Methodist missionary to the West Indies,
I crossed the Atlantic five times on beautiful ocean liners.
It was a magnificent adventure first as a
child and then a young teenager.

I am reminded of the man who saved up all his money
to buy a ticket to sail from England to New York City.
He bought his ticket but thought he had
no money left over for the meals,
so he packed a large suitcase with cheese and crackers.

Every mealtime, while the other passengers would go into the vast,
luxuriously appointed dining room, eating superlative meals,
this man would sit outside eating his cheese and crackers.

Towards the end of the voyage another man came and said to him,
"I notice that at meal times you sit and eat cheese and crackers.
Why don't you come into the dining room
and eat with the rest of us?"
The man replied, "I only had enough money to buy the boat ticket
and have nothing left over for the meals."

The man smiled and said,
"Don't you know the meals are included in the ticket price?"

All the time the man had the opportunity of eating
an already "paid for" sumptuous meal,
but chose to eat "cheese and crackers".

This is a perfect illustration of how we
approach God's purpose for us.
In Christ, the price has already been paid for
the sumptuous blessings that are ours,
laid out in God's purpose for us.
Yet because the "soil" of our lives is not cultivated and receptive
to that special seed prepared for us,
we choose instead a "cheese and crackers" lifestyle!

Go beyond "cheese and crackers"!

Too many of us have no idea how to receive
our "paid for" sumptuous meal.
We ask: "How is it possible to receive God's blessings?
We have made a commitment to Christ as Lord of our lives,
but we don't know how to go any further."

The answer is:
Stand in agreement with God's promises
to each of us with thanksgiving.

Receiving God's blessings does not come through understanding
the "How?" or the "When?"

but by tenaciously believing in faith
that God's promises are there for the asking and the receiving.

We make spiritual principles and promises so complicated,
seeking to understand the process and rationale of how God works,
that we miss their manifestations in our lives!

Acceptance comes before understanding!

Believing God's promises are for us is the key to receiving them.
We may wrestle in our minds with the "How?" and the "When?";
there will be those around us who will scoff at our "simple, naive
faith" and try to fill our minds and hearts with negative thoughts.

But Jesus stated the process:
"Whatever we ask we receive from Him." [21]

Receive God's best blessings by opening our hearts in trusting faith;
speaking words of thanksgiving for the
goodness and greatness of God
and His promises for us.

Beware the "joy stealers"!

Resist negative people.
Avoid those who only speak their complaints
about life and their circumstances!
They are the "joy stealers"!
If you let them,
they will steal your joy and block God's
blessings from flowing into your life!

Some would and will say, "That's naïve!"

We respond:
"We walk by faith, not by sight!" [22]

We choose to believe God and take Him at His Word!
We choose to stand with Abraham who believed in God,
**"…and calls those things which do not exist
as though they did."** [23]

God promised Abraham that he would
be the "father of many nations".
That was the literal meaning of his name, "Abraham".
He believed God, even though "realistically"
speaking that was a physical impossibility.
Can you imagine the smiles and smirks that
must have been on people's faces
when Abraham introduced himself to them by name?
"Father of many nations"!
You must be joking! You're too old! You don't even have a son!

Yet as Paul wrote in Romans:
"And not being weak in faith,
he did not consider his own body, already dead…
and the deadness of Sarah's womb.
He did not waver at the promise of God through unbelief,
but was strengthened in faith, giving glory to God,
and being fully convinced that what He had promised
He was also able to perform." [24]

**Don't focus on your circumstance!
Focus on the goodness and greatness of God
and believe His promises for your life!**

Find in Scripture His specific promise for
you and start giving thanks to God,
receiving that promise by faith not understanding.
Then begin feasting in God's dining room,
leaving behind your "cheese and crackers"
and live out your divine purpose with passion!

Let the feasting begin!

"CHRIST IN YOU, THE HOPE OF GLORY!"
(Colossians 1:27, NKJV)

"AND NOT BEING WEAK IN FAITH,
HE DID NOT CONSIDER HIS OWN BODY,
ALREADY DEAD…
AND THE DEADNESS OF
SARAH'S WOMB.
HE DID NOT WAVER AT THE PROMISE
OF GOD THROUGH UNBELIEF,
BUT WAS STRENGTHENED IN FAITH,
GIVING GLORY TO GOD,
AND BEING FULLY CONVINCED
THAT WHAT HE
HAD PROMISED
HE WAS ALSO ABLE TO PERFORM."
(Romans 4:19, NKJV)

"YOUR DREAM LIES IN THE
DIRECTION
OF AN OVERWHELMING OBSTACLE.
IF YOU GO TOWARD IT TODAY,
YOU WILL BRING GOD HONOR.
AND YOU WILL EXPERIENCE
A LIFE MARKED
BY MIRACLES
AS GOD INTERVENES ON
YOUR BEHALF."

CHAPTER 9

THE PASSION FOR PATIENCE

H.G. Wells has a satirical short story about an
Archbishop who encountered a difficulty
and decided to pray about it.
He had always said his prayers regularly.
He regarded prayer as a purifying, beneficial process,
no more to be neglected than brushing his teeth.
Yet he never really asked God for anything.
He had not made a particular and personal
appeal to God for many years.

In this difficulty, however, he needed help desperately and so,
entering his private chapel, he sank to his
knees and folded his hands.
"O God," he began and paused.
Then he heard a voice - a clear strong voice.
"Yes," said the voice, "What is it?"
They found his Grace the next morning.
He had slipped off the chancel steps and lay
sprawling on the crimson carpet.
Plainly his death had been instantaneous.

How many of us would die of fright if we ever heard a voice
responding to our prayers, saying, "Yes, what is it?"
How many of us expect God to reveal His
guidance for our lives when we pray?
Most of our praying is simply a one-sided 'communication'.

The fact is, however, that if we are really
listening and responding to God
we can expect to hear and recognize the 'voice'.

God has a perfect plan for our lives.
Our challenge, despite our circumstances and our past failures,
which would shackle us,
is to stand firm in that belief in God's plan
and then act on the "leadings",
the "nudges", sent by the Spirit.

Abraham Lincoln makes this point quite clearly when he said,
"I am satisfied that when the Almighty wants
me to do, or not do any particular thing,
He finds a way of letting me know."

God had a perfect plan for Lincoln's life
and Lincoln refused to allow his "defeats" to
shackle him from achieving that plan.
Look at his life:
As a young man Abraham Lincoln went to
the Black Hawk War a captain and,
through no fault of his own, returned a private.
That brought an end to his military career.
Then his little shop in a country village
"winked out", as he used to say,
marking his failure as a businessman.
As a lawyer in Springfield, Illinois, he was
too impractical, too unpolished,
too temperamental, to be a success.

Turning to politics,
he was defeated in his first campaign for the legislature,
defeated in his first attempt to be nominated for Congress,

defeated in his application to be Commissioner
of the General Land Office,
defeated in the Senatorial Election of 1854,
defeated in his aspirations for the Vice-Presidency in 1856,
defeated again in the Senatorial Election of 1858.
Yet 1861 found him in the White House
as President of the United States.

How did Lincoln interpret this strange
succession of failures and frustrations
which finally culminated in terrific personal victory?
He stated, "That the Almighty directly intervenes in human affairs
is one of the plainest statements in the Bible.
I have had so many evidences of His direction,
so many instances when I have been controlled
by some other Power than my own will,
that I have no doubt but what this Power comes from above."

Whatever our present circumstances and past defeats,
God still has a perfect plan for us as we truly
seek Him and listen for His voice.
This belief fuels our **hope**, and that attitude
of hope changes everything!
It is the beginning of patient expectation!

At an International Psychiatric Congress in Madrid, Spain,
one of the main lectures was on the healing power of hope.
Renowned psychiatrists from all over the
world gathered to discuss and agree
that the single most important healing force is hope:
hope of recovery, hope of loving and being loved,
hope of making it, hope of succeeding.

One speaker turned the word "hope" into this acronym:
Hold On Praying Expectantly!

Sometimes we talk about God's Blessing,
but in reality the word "blessing" has become so
diluted by misuse that it has lost its force.
It's something we say when someone sneezes.
It has become so vague and innocuous that the phrase "Bless you!"
has become equivalent to "Have a nice day!"

But "to bless" in the Biblical sense means to ask
for, or to impart supernatural favour.
When we ask for God's blessing,
we're not asking for more of what we could get for ourselves.
We're crying out for the wonderful, unlimited goodness
that only God has the power to know about, or give to us.

With this attitude, God's power to accomplish
great things finds no obstruction in us,
and the unhindered forces of heaven can begin
to accomplish God's perfect plan for us.
As we stand steadfast in this belief,
God will bring the right people, at the right
time, with the right opportunities
into our lives to establish His plan.

Patience is steadfast endurance!

We stand steadfast in our faith holding on, praying expectantly.
Quitting is not in our vocabulary!
Nor do we set limits on the power of God to act on our behalf.

I read how a pastor met with a group of
hundreds of university students
from twelve nations.
It happened during the last week of an intense
month long initiative in Swaziland,

where these young people had spent a full week visiting
every single high school in the nation to teach abstinence
as the primary method for HIV prevention.
The students glowingly shared remarkable
and even miraculous stories
of what God had done during that week.

When it was his turn to speak, he shared a
major concern facing his faith-based
humanitarian organization.
They had set their goal of recruiting ten
thousand American volunteers
to come to Africa during the next year,
but were told by the airlines that travel
arrangements on this scale would be
problematic.

So he asked the students to join with them and pray
that God would provide the organization with a 747 jet.
Laughter erupted across the room as the
students shook their heads in disbelief.

The pastor posed this question to the audience:
"Let's say you had run out of money and
needed funds to buy food to eat.
So you prayed and asked God to supply as He promised.
Or let's say that you had run out of seats and needed a 747
to carry thousands of volunteers to Africa.
So you prayed and asked God to supply as He promised.

Which would be more difficult for God
to provide, the food or the 747?
Would He say, "The food is no problem, and
maybe I can find you a four seater.
But a 747, you've got to be joking?"

The silence in the room shouted that the students
had seen the root of their unbelief.
One thing was not harder than another for God.

God doesn't know the word "HARD"!

Two nights later, at midnight, the pastor's phone rang.
It was a friend from the States.
He said a corporation that wished to remain anonymous
had decided to purchase a 747 jet for the organization.

The truth is, the hand of God is always available to us.
Yet, as with us today, many people in Biblical
times thought that the power of God
was no longer available in their day.
The challenge for us is to move out of our
"comfort zones" and security
and take the risk of faith, giving God a
chance to demonstrate His power.
As we step out in faith, He will show up!

**The walk of faith insists that we are expected
to attempt something large enough
that failure is guaranteed...
unless God steps in!**

When we stand fast in faith,
holding on praying expectantly,
God is then able to release His power to accomplish His will,
receiving the glory through solving all those seeming impossibilities.
God is watching and waiting for us to ask for
the supernatural power He offers:

**"For the eyes of the LORD run to and
fro throughout the whole earth,**

**to show Himself strong on behalf of those
whose heart is loyal to Him."** [1]

Unlike our approach,
God is not scanning the horizon for spiritual
giants or highly talented men and women.
Rather, He is eagerly seeking those who are sincerely loyal to Him.
Our "loyal heart" is the only part of His
expansion plan that He will not provide.
It is our responsibility to make Him our primary commitment.

A pastor was leading fifty leaders who
supervised the work of thousands
of Christian workers all around the world.
They were grouped around seven tables and asked
to brain-storm the three biggest reasons
why we are not seeing God's power being released.

After ten minutes, the pastor asked the first table,
"What's your number one reason?"
The answer, "Unbelief".

When he asked them to explain, they replied,
"We may pray, but we don't really believe
that God is going to intervene,
that He wants to intervene,
or that He even has the power."

He asked the second table the same question.
They answered, "Unbelief."
The room became quiet.
This was shocking because they hadn't been discussing unbelief.
Table three: "Unbelief".
Table four: "Unbelief".

And on it went.

Table six listed unbelief as the second reason.

Every other group had placed it at the top of their list.

The hand of God is blocked by our unbelief!

We may believe in some form that God is active in our world
and in the lives of some people,
but when it comes to our own lives there is no passionate conviction
because our experience does not manifest that power.

Why?

Yes, there is unbelief, but it's more.
It's the easy decision to quit on our faith
when God doesn't act immediately!
This is where we need the passion of patience!
Patience and quitting are incompatible!

If we are to develop real passion in our Christian faith
we need both a proper understanding and a
personal application of "patience".
In our age of "instant gratification" and advanced technology,
patience is not one of the most highly prized virtues.
When we want something, we want it NOW!

We also misunderstand the real meaning of "patience".
We think of it as being little more than the
ability to tolerate a bad situation
without complaint,
as a kind of spiritual consolation prize we ask God for
when we can't seem to get what we really want.

If we think of patience in this way we miss its
deep meaning and relevance for us!
Patience **DOES NOT** mean settling sweetly for the second best.
It **DOES NOT** mean standing by meekly
while trouble tramples our lives.

"PATIENCE" IS A POWER WORD!

The New Testament meaning of "patience",
as literally translated from the Greek,
is "to be consistently constant",
or "to be the same way all the time, regardless of what happens."

Consistently constant!

We have deleted the tenacious power of patience
by relegating it to a "passive" virtue,
stripping it of its virile application!
When we are going through tough times, we
stand on God's promises with patience,
standing "consistently constant",
maintaining our faith in those promises
until they are manifest in our lives.

James writes:
"My brethren, count it all joy when you fall into various trials,
knowing that the testing of your faith produces patience.
But let patience have its perfect work,
that you may be perfect and complete, lacking nothing.
If any of you lacks wisdom, let him ask of God,
who gives to all liberally and without
reproach, and it will be given to him.
But let him ask in faith, with no doubting,

for he who doubts is like a wave of the sea
driven and tossed by the wind.
For let not that man suppose that he will
receive anything from the Lord;
he is a double-minded man, unstable in all his ways." [2]

James is saying, in effect,
be relentlessly consistent in staying focused on
God and His promises for your life.
Let nothing distract you from your passionate
patience as you wait for God's answers.
Do not let doubt infect your mind.
When the questions of "How?", "When?" and "Why?" come up,
slam the door and keep them out!

In consistency lies the power!

The victory lies in consistently confessing the Word of God
in the face of every negative circumstance.
The audacity of faith proclaims:

"Let God be true but every man a liar." [3]

No matter what challenges you face, and however long it takes,
let nothing shake you in standing firm on God's promise for you.

This tremendous illustration of a man in
Akron, Ohio, illustrates the point.
The man was a soldier in the 1930's, when the
U.S. government was experimenting
with dirigibles (airships).
He was assigned along with 200 other
soldiers to help move an airship
that had landed in Akron.

Imagine moving a giant zeppelin like the
Hindenburg and you will get the picture.
At first, the job seemed simple enough.
All they had to do was tie the dirigible with ropes to a steel tower
so that it wouldn't float away.
As the soldiers were holding the ropes, however,
something unexpected happened.
The dirigible started going up.

Some of the men had the presence of mind to let go of the ropes.
But others didn't.
They kept holding on as the airship rose in the air.
For a while, they dangled in the sky,
clinging to the ropes for dear life.
But eventually, as bystanders watched in
horror, they began to lose their grip.

People screamed, children cried, as one by
one the men fell to the ground.
Some sustained serious injuries - others died.
Eventually all eyes turned toward one last man.
He was hanging so high in the air he looked like a toy soldier.
People stared, holding their breath, expecting him to fall.
But he didn't.
Time passed.
He just can't keep holding on, they thought.
More time passed.
Any minute now he will fall!
But still, he held on.

Finally, the man was rescued.
Certain he'd need medical attention after his harrowing ordeal;
officials brought in an ambulance and rushed
to meet him with a stretcher.

He just waved it away.
"I'm all right," he told them.
"But you're bound to be exhausted!" they said.

"No," replied the man.
"When I saw I was too far away from the earth to let go,
I held on with one hand,
threw about four feet of the rope around
me, and tied it," he explained.
"I didn't hold the rope.
It held me."

"That's the way we live the faith life!
That's how we hang in there with patience until
we receive that for which we're believing.
Instead of holding onto God's promises
with our own human strength,
we let the divine power within the promises hold us.
We wrap ourselves in the Word and swing free!"

Don't speak against your blessing!

While you wait in patience,
being consistently constant,
never allow any negative words to come out of your lips,
or negative thoughts contaminate your mind.

As Paul wrote to the Romans:
**"Do not be conformed to this world,
but be transformed by the renewing of your mind."** [4]

That renewal of our minds makes the radical
world shift from "sight" to "faith".
The world maintains: "I'll believe it when I see it!"

But the person of faith stands with patience,
"seeing with the eye of faith",
waiting expectantly for the manifestation.

One writer states: "Satan works on you
the same way he worked on Eve.
He tries to discredit God's Word in your mind…
Deception is all he has to use against the Body of Christ…
Satan wants your words!
In order to be successful,
he has to deceive you into speaking words that will stop your faith."

As we wait for the answer to our prayer,
we stand in confident, expectant faith.
And God will often surprise us with the
manifestation of his answers.
Just because you don't see a way doesn't
mean that God doesn't have a way.

I recall this amusing yet true story of Lindsey
who desperately wanted a kitten.
Her parents refused but, out of frustration, her mother said,

"If God gives you a kitten I'll let you keep it.
But we're not buying one."

Lindsey had the trusting faith of a little child
and so she went out into the backyard,
got down on her knees, and said,
"God, I'm asking you to please give me a kitten."

When she finished praying with her mother watching over her,
all of a sudden out of nowhere a kitten came flying out of the sky
and landed a few feet away.

The mother couldn't believe her eyes. She
thought she was seeing things.
There was no tree overhead.
It looked like the kitten had fallen from the heavens.

Lindsey picked it up and said, "Look,
Mommy. God gave me my kitten."
The mother stood there dumbfounded in disbelief.

Several months later the mother learned what had happened.
The neighbours who lived behind her and
a few houses down the road
were trying to get this little kitten out of a tree,
but the tree was too tall for the man to reach with his ladder.
So the man tied a rope to the tree,
and he hooked the rope to the back of his car.

He started slowly pulling forward in the car to bend the tree over.
Just when the tree bent low enough to reach the kitten,
the rope slipped and the tree acted like a slingshot.

It slung that kitten nearly two hundred yards
and it fell right at that little girl's feet.
That man felt terrible.
No one could find the kitten. He thought it was dead.
He didn't know that he'd answered a little girl's prayer.
God works in mysterious ways.

While that true story may be humorous and seem far-fetched,
being "consistently constant" in our faith in God's
promises does bring amazing results.
It is patience having her perfect work
bringing about God's answers.

George Mueller of Bristol, England founded
a series of orphanages and,
rather than asking for donations and seeking financial help,
he patiently waited with confidence on God to be his Source
in meeting his needs for these children.

One evening he sat at his dinner table,
as he did every night surrounded by these orphan children,
there was no food for them to eat.
The table was set, but the plates in front of the children were empty.

But Mueller, with a faith-filled face, said:
"Let's do what we've always done."
In this crisis of a circumstance they prayed together.
They prayed a prayer of thanksgiving to God
for what the Lord would provide.
In addition, Mueller thanked the Lord for how he would give and,
when he said "Amen", the children lifted their heads
and looked at his stern but confident face radiating faith.

A knock came at the door and Mueller asked
one of the orphans to answer the door.
The boy turned and said,
"Mr. Mueller, it's the vegetable man and he has some vegetables."
The man said, "These vegetables will wilt if we don't give them away
and I apologize for presuming on you and the orphans,
but I thought you could use them."

As he was speaking and unloading his truck,
another knock came and it was the butcher,
who said to Mr. Mueller,
"I've run out of ice and salt and I thought
if I didn't unload this meat,
it would go to waste.

So I thought I'd see if there was any use
for this meat at your orphanage."

Before he could finish, another knock came.

It was the milkman who said, "I've filled more quarts than needed
and I had some milk left over
and I thought I'd bring it to you and see if you could use it."
Needless to say, Mueller's orphanage that
night had more than enough.
It was a grand banquet on the scale of God.
Everything they needed God had wonderfully supplied.

**Don't speak against your blessing in doubt for
God will make a way where there seems to be no way!**

Another writer states:
"The first step in defeating Satan's attack against you
is to make the decision that you are not going to allow him
to change your confession of faith that you
believe you received when you prayed.
Make an irrevocable decision of these things:

God's Word is true.
I will act only in faith.
I will speak only in faith.
I have believed I receive

This confident attitude comes from a Word-ruled mind.
**Casting down arguments and every high thing
that exalts itself against the knowledge
of God, bringing every thought
into captivity to the obedience of Christ.** [5]

The decision of your will -
to stand and continue to stand, regardless of
the enemy's tactics and pressure –
will enable you to accomplish the will of
God and receive what is promised.
Your decision will cause the power of
patience to undergird your faith.
Patience is the quality that does not surrender to circumstances.

Patience operates at **your** will.
It does not operate for you at anyone else's will, not even God's.
You determine your will in a situation.

Never waver!

.Refuse to speak words contrary to what
you believe you have received.
Continually speak the Word of God into the face of adversity.
The enemy is after your words so that he can use them against you.
Refuse to let him influence your words.
Speak words of faith.
Speak the end result.
Speak words of success.
Speak words of abundance.
Speak words of healing.
You will have what you say.
Make your words agree with what you desire
to come to pass and God will act.

Patience = Tenacity!

American psychiatrist, Dr. Smiley Blaton,
stated that one of the greatest truths in the
Bible was Paul's word in Ephesians:
"And having done all to stand…Stand therefore!" [6]

In modern language Paul would say,
after you have done your best, don't quit!

What trial is testing your faith right now?
It may be that you've been looking for a job and can't find one;
it may be financial pressure, health defects, or relationship issues.
Whatever the challenge,
we are all called to stand on the promise
of God as it relates to our need
and wait with expectant faith and patience for its manifestation!

In the time between standing on God's
promise and its manifestation,
it will be easy to become discouraged and be tempted to quit, saying
"Faith doesn't work!"
But as the writer to the Hebrews states:

**"Therefore do not cast away your confidence,
which has great reward.
For you have need of endurance,
So that, after you have done the will of God,
you may receive the promise."** [7]

<u>**Don't bend to the pressure of time!**</u>

There may be a significant period of time
between your claiming God's promise for
your life and its manifestation,
but resist the temptation to quit.

FACING THE GIANTS is a movie created by
a small Baptist Church in Georgia, USA,
and then Sony made it into a full screen movie.
It has a powerful Christian message.

It's the story of a losing football team that's
going down the drain in a big way.
The coach is trying to motivate the losing
team to give their very best.

He lined them all up in the end zone, put his finger
in the face of the best athlete and said,
"I want you to give me the very best you have!"
They had been doing a "crab crawl" with someone on their backs.
They had been going about ten to fifteen yards.
That was about all they could do.

So the coach looked at this young athlete and
said, "Can you give me your very best?
Do you think you can crawl thirty yards?"
He replied, "I'll try."
So the football coach got him down on all fours, blindfolded him,
put another man on his back and he started crab crawling.

When the athlete got to the point where he was used to giving up
the coach got down next to his ear and shouted:
"I want your best! Keep going!"
He kept going and kept going and when he got tired the coach said,
"Don't even think of quitting, you've got more left! Keep going!"

And he kept going, and kept going, and when he finally stopped
the coach took the blindfold off and the young athlete saw
he had crawled the whole length of the football
field and was in the other end zone!

The faith application for us is very simple.
When we think we can't go any further
the Master gets down beside us and whispers in our ears, you
"…can do all things through Christ who strengthens…." [8]

God will never allow us to be tested beyond our capacity!
We then feel motivated to pick it up and go a little further
and we can keep on persevering in the fight for we believe,
"He who is in you is greater than he who is in the world." [9]

Suddenly we stop whining and start becoming
warriors because we know:
"If God is for us, who can be against us?" [10]

There is no limitation in God!

When we are struggling with our faith in tough times,
we are not to be "double minded",
swinging this way and that in our convictions.
Rather, we are to stand fast with tenacious patience
fully convinced that what God has promised
will come to pass in our lives!
How long do we have to stand waiting for
God's promise to be manifest?
As one writer stated, **"If we are prepared to
stand forever, it won't be long!"**
What happens when adversity comes?
God's promises are as true today as they were in the past.
The God of our history is the God of our destiny!
Our response to trials should be this:
Faith opens the door to God's promises to us
and Patience keeps that door open
until the promise is manifested.
Without the tenacity of patience, the door will
slam shut at the first sign of trouble.
So to do this, we personally harness the power of God!

The God of our history is the God of our destiny!

We don't doubt God's power,
but what trips us up is HOW does that power
flow into our personal challenges?

For Biblical examples of this we go back
to that pivotal manifestation
of God's delivering power
in the Exodus story.
Following the tenth plague,
which was the visitation of the angel of death on Egypt,
Pharaoh let the Israelites go –
and go they did, with nearly all of the wealth of Egypt.

Pharaoh mobilized 600 of his finest chariots to go after them,
not because of the loss of cheap slave labour,
but because of the money they had taken with them!
The Egyptian economy was headed into a tailspin.
They soon caught up with the snail paced
migration of the Israelites and,
when the Israelites realized what was happening –
the fact that they were caught between the
Egyptian army and the Red Sea –
they fell apart in front of Moses.

In response to their panic in Exodus 14 Moses said in effect:
"Everything's going to be all right.
I've got the word from God and His strength
is going to be applied to our situation.
God's given us the order to march towards the Red Sea
and He will intervene somewhere between here and there."

It's easy to imagine the dilemma faced by the Israelites.
There's an army behind you, and God says,
"Keep walking towards the uncrossable Red Sea and, as you do,

I will honor your faith by a display of my power.
You're not going to see it now, but my promise is:
Power along the way!

Moses says to the people:
"Do not be afraid.
Stand still, and see the salvation of the LORD,
which He will accomplish for you today.
For the Egyptians whom you see today,
you shall see again no more forever.
The Lord will fight for you, and you shall hold your peace." [11]

God delivers the Israelites and they cross through the Red Sea,
but it certainly took real faith to believe in
the intervening power of God
before the manifestation.
We, like the Israelites, would always prefer
"power before the problem";
power before the crisis gets too intense;
power before we reach the water's edge –
but God doesn't work that way.

God delivered exactly what He promised to deliver:
Power, but "power along the way".

One would have thought that such deliverance would be
indelibly carved into their consciousness causing total
faith in God's ability to deliver on all His promises.

Not so and, in their rebellion against God,
nearly all of the escapees were punished for their disobedience
and were never allowed to enter the Promised Land.

We move to the stage when the Israelites
are about to cross the Jordan
and finally enter the Promised Land.
The previous generation had died in the wilderness
and this is a new group of people
for whom the Red Sea experience is second hand.
Again they are called to trust God for their deliverance.

The Jordan River is in flood and the order from God is this:
Organize all the people in a long line.
Put the Ark of the Covenant at the front of the line
and make sure that everyone is following the Ark.
They are then commanded to move towards the churning,
swirling waters of the Jordan river in full flood.

For this generation of Israelites their faith
had to be supremely tested
for Joshua 3:15 says that the people in the
front of the line were ankle deep
before God miraculously parted the water.

Once again "power along the way!"

This is a sustaining image for those of us who stand
"ankle deep" in the cold, rushing water
of whatever problem we are facing as we
cry for God's delivering power!

In Hebrew, the word translated "I believe" also means "I remember".
In our faith walk we are called to remember
how God has demonstrated His power
in our lives in the past.
But, while we want "power before the problem",
God's pattern is "power along the way".

In The New Testament narrative in Luke, ten
lepers come to Jesus asking for healing.
He knows they're asking for divine healing and,
to their request, Jesus simply responds,
" 'Go, show yourselves to the priests.' " [12]
(the ones who would certify their cleansing)!"

Action of belief motivates the glory of healing!

It's easy to imagine the lepers looking at each other,
assuming they were going to be immediately healed, questioning:
"Do we have to go into the town to have the
priest tell us what we already know -
we're lepers?"
Perhaps one of them said,
"Suppose something miraculous happens between here and there?
Suppose Jesus wants to see if we have the faith to believe
that He will display His healing power
as we respond in obedience?"

"And so it was that as they went, they were cleansed." [13]

This illustrates the process of faith and obedient patience!
We all want power before the problem,
but Jesus calls us to the faith which receives "power along the way".
Yes, He can heal instantly,
but often His promise demands obedience
and patience before manifestation!

Robert Raines puts it this way when he describes
the Biblical journey of Abraham.
"Abraham and Sarah had no map to the promised land,
no inside track to discover the land of their inheritance.
All they had was the promise of a presence on the journey."

So it is with us.
In our journey we discover again that Biblical
faith is not all about knowledge.
Faith is commitment without all the evidence being in.
Faith is learning to trust God in the dark.
Faith is risk as well as promise,
and darkness in the tunnel
as well as the hope of light at the end of the tunnel.

A Rabbi makes this point:
"It's interesting to note, according to the Jewish calendar,
that the day begins at sundown, not at sunup.
All festivals and holy days begin at night.
The Sabbath begins at sundown."

According to Jewish tradition, this is of moral significance.
It is not difficult to have confidence in the day
and to believe in the existence of light at sunup.
The Jewish day begins at night to symbolize the faith,
even in darkness,
that light will prevail and that a new day will dawn upon mankind.

This is our faith that even in the darkness
we believe in God's promises.
Paul writes:
"Finally…be strong in the Lord, and in the power of His might.
Put on the whole armor of God, that you may be able to
stand against the wiles of the devil.

For we do not wrestle against flesh and blood,
but against principalities, against powers,
against the rulers of the darkness of this age,
against spiritual hosts of wickedness in the heavenly places.

Therefore take up the whole armor of God,
that you may be able to withstand
in the evil day, and having done all,
to stand." [14]

When we start to fuss and fume about some
difficulty we are to stand still and affirm:

**God is still on the throne,
His promises are still good.
Stand firm until we receive them!**

Too often we've allowed our feelings and desire for understanding
to take over in the times of trial
and, in so doing, we short-circuit the process
of God's actions in our lives.
The challenge is to stop this downward spiral and
refuse to let our thoughts and feelings
take us into anger, despondency, doubt and fear,
and finally into failure.

Patience stops that downward spiral before it starts!
James is saying this to us:
Toughen up your faith with patience!

Just because God's delivering power is
not coming on your timetable,
does not mean it won't come to pass!
What He has promised will come to pass
if we stand firm in our belief that we will receive!

We used to hear this phrase quite often from our elders:
"Possess your souls in patience!"

That's the correct antidote to modern
attitudes of "instant gratification".
As one writer puts it: "If you'll let patience have her perfect work,
if you'll remain consistently constant,
trusting in and relying confidently on the Word of God,
you'll end up perfect and complete, wanting nothing."

**Patience is the power that puts God's
promises within your reach!**

All that I have been sharing with you in these
chapters comes together in the life of my close
friend Maureen, a lady of passionate faith.
Some months after the death of her husband
she began to experience severe digestive problems.
The problem increased in severity for some six
weeks as she lost considerable weight,
coming down to a fraction of her full physical health.

Every day she would have to deal with the
inability to keep any nourishment down,
often having to stop at awkward times to throw
up what little remained in her stomach.

From a very strong woman she now emerged with increasing frailty,
until finally her brother literally carried her
to a hospital emergency ward.
There she underwent tests which revealed stomach cancer.

**Despite the outward circumstances,
she stood fast on God's promise of healing!**

She went home to consider the implications of the operation
which had been immediately scheduled for her by the oncologist.

But her sister-in-law, who worked in a
surgical unit in another hospital
suggested she get a second opinion.
This she did, and once more was told that
tests revealed stomach cancer,
and an operation was scheduled two weeks later.

At that point, Maureen, with her tenacious
belief in the promises of God for her life,
contacted seven good friends who were
mature in intercessory prayer.
She told them of her condition but insisted
that she did not "have" cancer,
but rather that the doctors "had found" cancer in her stomach.
She refused to take ownership of the disease.
So they joined in prayer for healing.

Four nights before the scheduled surgery,
Maureen lay praying in bed when she heard the
words in her spirit: "Read Psalm 30".
She reached for her Bible and found the Psalm and read
**"O Lord my God, I cried out to You,
And you healed me."** [15]

The words of the entire Psalm portrayed the
feelings she had been going through
for the past weeks.
At that moment she felt healed in her body.

She, who previously could scarcely drink a small glass of juice,
could now digest small amounts of solid food and keep it down.
As she gained in strength she asked the Lord what she should do
about the scheduled operation.
The word she received in her spirit was:
"You are under authority of the doctor".

So she entered the hospital for the scheduled surgery
but told the doctor that she had been healed
and that he would find no evidence of cancer in her stomach.
She agreed to the operation believing that this
testimony would give glory to God.
To the complete astonishment of the surgical
team, when they operated they found,
as she had predicted, no evidence of cancer.

The previous tests from both hospitals were re-examined and,
once again, evidence of cancer showed up on the results.
But the operation revealed the manifestation
of God's promise of healing.

The cynic might say this was simply coincidence
or some such dismissive comment,

but to this woman of faith it was a vindication of
the belief that she had received the promise
of the Lord to which she had held so tenaciously.

**In the face of all the "evidence" she knew how to live
The Power of Passion!**

And in that she is an example for us all!

CHAPTER 10

THE PASSION FOR POWER

Many of us can believe in the transforming power of faith
but the persistent question is:
"How can I have that power?"
Scripture tells us that "faith works by
love" and so the issue should be:
if I can only love myself and others then the
power of faith would be mine.
But how do I learn to love?

Countless books have been written to
answer this perennial question,
but the answer is often far more complex that one would suspect.
Too often the focus of the question has been on the individual
and the various issues basic to that individual's development.
But the focus is wrong!
The answer to the "power of faith" is found in centering ourselves,
not on ourselves, but on God;
focusing not on our love, but on God's love!

Paul outlines the characteristics of love in his
First letter to the Corinthians, chapter 13,
but the definition of love is I John 4:10, NKJV:
"In this is love, not that we loved God,
but that He loved us,
and sent His Son to be the propitiation for our sins." [1]

Love is defined, then, not as our love for God, but His love for us.
And yet how many times have we been challenged,
by ourselves or in churches,
"You've got to love God more."
All the while saying within ourselves,
"How do I do that?"

The fact is that, for most of us, we are not
desperately in love with God.
God's grace shows us that it is not **my** love for God that is the issue,
but God's love for me!
So we love, not because we love God,
but because He first loved us!
Our focus every day should not be on **our** love for God -
that is the debilitating introspection where
we keep asking ourselves:
"Am I loving God enough?"
Imagine your child having that attitude towards you?
"Am I loving Daddy or Mummy enough?"
That attitude is neurotic and self-centered.

Rather, imagine a huge magnifying glass over your head
with God's love shining on you!
Then we experience the presence of the
overwhelming power of His love.

We affirm God's love for us as we affirm with the Apostle Paul:
"...the Son of God, who loved me and gave himself for me." [2]
The more we sense that, not our love for God, but His love for us,
the more we will be empowered to love,
because He first loved us!

The issue for too many of us is that we focus
on our behaviour, on our "works".

**That introspection is dangerous because
it keeps us self-occupied!**
There's nothing more pitiable and debilitating
than being self-occupied.
God wants us to be Christ-occupied!

We can now say to God,
"Now I know how much you love me,
for you didn't hold back your only Son, the Son whom You love."
We will never know how much God loves us,
until we know how much God loves Jesus,
because God gave Jesus up for us!

**Perfect love is not our love for God for
that love can never be perfect!**
Perfect love is God's love for us and that
perfect love will cast out every fear,
when we see it,
when we believe it,
when we practice it.
Practicing the love of God means developing that
intimate awareness which is able to shout and
rejoice in the very depths of our beings:
"I AM GOD'S BELOVED!"

When we read and believe that God gave up
His Son for us, His only beloved Son,
we become overwhelmed by the love of God.
**Then we are set free from all our striving to be worthy
and we are then open to receive.**

It is true that "faith works through love", but the
mistake is in thinking that it means I need to
love you more and more in order for my faith to work.

Not so!
Faith works by realizing how much God loves me;
then I can love others through the revelation
and empowerment of His love!

**"Love has been perfected among us in this:
that we may have boldness in the day of judgement;
because as He is, so are we in this world."** [3]

The implication for us in this statement is astounding!
"As Jesus is, so are we IN THIS WORLD."
God is not looking at us to judge us.
God is looking at the perfect Son at His right hand to judge us.
"As He us, so are we in this world."

It's not a question of: "Am I pleasing to God?"
It's the question: "Is Christ pleasing to God?"

Is Christ under God's unclouded favour today?
Yes. So are we in this world.
Is God's light shining on His Son at His right hand?
Yes! So are we in this world.
Can Jesus at the Father's right hand ever
come into condemnation again?
No! So are we in this world.

But some people will say, "Let's be practical."
'As He is, so are we in this world' is not practical.
Tell me something to do!

Scripture tells us this:
"We all, with unveiled face beholding as in
a mirror the glory of the Lord,
are being transformed into the same image from glory to glory,
just as by the Spirit of the Lord." [4]

We are transformed, not by struggling, but by beholding!

On one occasion the disciples were on a boat in
the middle of a storm on the Sea of Galilee.
Peter looked up and saw Jesus walking on the water.
Imagine the scene:
Jesus walking on the water in the middle of
boisterous winds and high waves.
Peter looked at Jesus and said,
" 'Lord, if it is You, command me to come to You on the water.'
So He said, 'Come'. " [5]

And Peter stepped out in the middle of the
storm and walked towards Jesus.
Because as Peter saw Jesus as He is, Peter became supernatural.
He forgot about himself and was doing the impossible.
He was on top of his circumstances.

Then the devil came and said, "Hey, Peter this is not scientific!
You ought not to be walking on the water!"
Peter started looking around and saw the
high waves and boisterous wind.
Now, if there was no storm and a perfect calm,
do you think you can walk on the water?
The storm has nothing to do with it.
But the moment Peter took his eyes off Jesus;
Peter became natural and began to sink.

The message is basic:
Keep your eyes on Jesus and see God's goodness and love!

The enemy wants you to look at yourself!

He comes to you and says:
Look at your sin. You've done this wrong.
Look at your wrong thoughts.

The enemy is always causing us to look around
at various areas of our lives and even when we do right he says:
"This person reads 10 chapters of the
Bible a day; you only read one.
They pray five hours a day, you only pray for one minute."
**Even if you do right, it is not enough. He
is the accuser of the brethren.
It's never enough!
NEVER!**

**What God wants you to do is to look away from yourself
and say to the enemy:
"If you want to check me out, LOOK AT JESUS!
As He is, so am I in this world."**

A pastor tells how he preached a message on
this verse and unbeknownst to him
there was a woman in the congregation who would
undergo a physical challenge that week.
She went for a mammogram and found she had lumps in her breast.
The doctors were concerned and wanted her
back for further tests the next week.

She heard that message and listened to it again and again.
She wrote on her medical notes:
"As Jesus is, so am I in this world."
Then she added these words and showed them to her pastor.
"Jesus, do you have lumps in your breast?
As you are so am I in this world - free of lumps."

She went back to the doctor and they did
test after test and found nothing.
Transformed from glory to glory by the Spirit
of the Lord - God our Healer!
Imagine the transformation which would take place in our lives
if we made that message central: "As He is, so am I in this world."
It is the job of the Holy Spirit to change
our hearts and circumstances.
We are transformed by beholding the Spirit of the Lord.
It is not by our own efforts!

Don't fall for the lies of the enemy.
Don't stand looking at yourself asking,
"Am I pleasing to my Father?"
If you do that you will be warped.
Look away from yourself to the man at the Father's right hand.
"As He is, so am I in this world."

Stop looking within and start looking without!
Many people are looking for the presence
of the Holy Spirit **in them,**
when they should be looking at the work of Christ outside them.
No one can measure the price God paid in His perfect love.
Scripture states:
**"He who did not spare His own Son, but
delivered Him up for us all,
how shall He not with Him also freely give us all things?"** [6]

Knowing this perfect love is what empowers our faith:
"...faith working through love." [7]

Not OUR love, but the perfect love of God revealed in us!
When we know and experience this truth we are
firmly on the path of empowering our faith

to achieve the great promises of God.

Be passionate about that experience!

**"Behold what manner of love the Father has bestowed on us,
that we should be called children of God!"** [8]

The overflowing dimension of God's love eludes us.
In our selfish and self-centered society, the
reality of God's love seems beyond belief,
leaving us skeptical that such love could apply to us.
Our society operates with an attitude of "What's in it for me?"
and we assume God operates in the same manner.
We read Biblical passages of God's unlimited
promises and unconditional love
wondering whether God would really
deal with us in such a manner.

There is a humorous story of a man at
an airport who bought a bag
of little doughnuts and a coffee.
All the tables were taken.
Finally, he saw a table where there was only one
man sitting down, so he went to the table,
put down his coffee and carry-on bag,
took off his coat and sat down.

Then he took a sip of his coffee,
reached over to pick up the bag of doughnuts on the table,
took one out and put the bag back down.
The man who was already at the table, stretched
over, picked up the bag of doughnuts,
took out a doughnut, pushed the bag back
across the table and smiled.

The other man just couldn't believe it!

He didn't know what to say because he was so surprised by the act.
It was obvious that the guy was not "quite there",
because people just don't do that sort of thing, especially in Britain.
But he thought he better not do anything, because
the other person might be violent.

He gave him one of those "If looks could kill"
looks, picked up the bag of doughnuts,
took out a doughnut, then put the bag near his coffee.

The other man stretched over, picked up the
bag, took another doughnut, smiled,
and pushed the bag back.
The other guy just couldn't believe it.
Then the man got up to leave.

He put on his coat, picked up the bag of doughnuts,
broke one in half which he put in his mouth,
put the other half back in the bag, pushed the
bag back towards the other man,
smiled, waved, and went to catch his plane.

The man thought, "I just can't believe it. I'm
not going to touch that doughnut."
Now he was really angry.

He looked at his watch, saw that it was
time for him to catch his flight,
got up, put on his coat, bent down to pick up his carry-on luggage,
and there, on top of his luggage, was HIS bag of doughnuts!

The man suddenly realized that the other
man was sharing his doughnuts,
when all the time he thought the man was stealing them!

It's easy to get the point.
Because of our own limited and conditional love,
we assume God operates in the same way.
We judge God's actions and attitudes by our own.
It's no wonder we cannot comprehend the
love of God while we live our lives
in self-centered, judgmental attitudes towards others.

There is an unimaginable generosity,
an incredible promise of the power of blessing,
coming to each one of us out of God's love
which seeks to meet our every need.
Going back to that humorous illustration,
God owns all the doughnuts!

He gives them freely to all who are in need and
who ask Him, expecting to receive them.
It's an attitude of unlimited, unconditional generosity
which is totally alien both to ourselves and our culture.

"Faith works by love".
This is the secret of the passion for faith-power.
Paul writes:

"…that out of his glorious, unlimited resources he will give
you the mighty inner strengthening of his Holy Spirit.
And I pray that Christ will be more and
more at home in your hearts,
living within you as you trust in him.
May your roots go down deep into the soil of God's marvelous love;

and may you be able to feel and understand,
as all God's children should,
how long, how wide, how deep, and how high his love really is;
and to experience this love for yourselves,
though it is so great that you will never see the
end of it or fully know or understand it.
And so at last you will be filled up with God himself.
Now glory be to God,
who by his mighty power at work within us
is able to do far more than
we would ever dare to ask or dream of –
infinitely beyond our highest prayers,
desires, thoughts, or hopes.
May he be given glory forever and ever through
endless ages because of his master plan of salvation
for the Church through Jesus Christ." [9]

**"Rooted and grounded in such love" is
the secret of powerful faith!**

Seize it, practice it, internalize it,
and in our passionate praise receive the blessings God has for us.

There is a classic story about a man who dies and goes to heaven.
St. Peter is waiting for him and gives him a tour.
Amid the splendour of the golden streets,
the man sees a building that looks like an enormous warehouse.

He asks to go in there, but St. Peter replies cautiously.
Finally, St. Peter lets the man inside
and there the man sees rows and rows filled
with shelves, floor to ceiling,
each neatly stacked with white boxes tied with red ribbons.

All the boxes are named.
The man asks excitedly if he has one.

St. Peter nods and the man rushes off to find his.
Looking inside, the man lets out a deep sigh, as
St. Peter has heard many, many times.
Because there inside the white box
was a list of all the blessings God wanted to give him while on earth,
but he had never asked, or he had asked, but his
lovelessness had blocked his receiving.

Blessings are received through love.
Why, then, choose to live without such
liberating, unconditional love,
taking upon ourselves the jobs of the Holy Spirit (to convict),
and the Father (to judge)?

"Love one another as I have loved you," [10]says Christ.

**That's the passion which releases God's
power and providence into our lives!**

God's perfect love reveals another integral dimension:
FORGIVENESS!
<u>**Without the power of forgiveness within us nothing happens!**</u>
<u>**Without forgiveness there is no passion for power!**</u>

We need to understand why Jesus places such
critical priority on the need to forgive.
In past generations numerous books have been
written about God's forgiving us,
but relatively few books written about how we
can and should forgive each other!
Yet the two themes are intimately intertwined.

Jesus knew that once we plant the seed of
unforgiveness in our hearts and minds
it begins to grow!
That seed does not remain static.
It begins to grow roots which extend into unforeseen
and otherwise impregnable areas of our lives.

A perceptive counselor states:
"Unforgiveness unchecked becomes a cancer in the soul."
It spreads!

Cancer does not stay where it originates in its primary location,
but spreads and infects other previously healthy organs.
The malignant cells eat up positive cells.

Unforgiveness begins to affect every area of our lives.
It does not remain centered on one incident;
it begins to affect all our relationships.

For example, if you are angry with your ex-
husband and you are re-married,
the moment your new husband does anything
that remotely reminds you
of where you have been, you over-react,
because it is speaking to other areas of your life.

Not only does it cause you to over-react, it also
causes you to build walls around yourself
preventing you from living your life to the fullest.

Unforgiveness fuels everything that is negative
Unforgiveness eats up your personality, your
creativity, your energy, your spirituality.
Unforgiveness has too high a price to pay to hold onto.

Those of us who have been hurt may believe that unforgiveness
protects us from being vulnerable and hurt again.
In reality it does the opposite.
Unforgiveness has everything to do with you
and nothing to do with the other person.

It's not as though if you don't forgive the other person
you're going to be protected from future hurts.
The worst part about it is:
not only does unforgiveness block you from
interacting with that person;
it blocks you from taking the risk of love and
you end up in a state of isolation;
you incarcerate yourself through unforgiveness.
Unforgiveness gives the other person the ability to rob you
not just for the moment they violated
you, but of your future as well.

**Unforgiveness is like drinking poison
and then expecting the person who has hurt you to die!**

Renowned oncologist, Dr Bernie Siegel, states:
"Feelings are chemical and can kill or cure."

Siegel emphasizes the unity of the mind and body and
illustrates this by their dramatic connection in the life of a
Filipino woman who in 1977 was cured of a serious disease
by a native healer, after Western medicine had failed her.

Suffering from systemic lupus erythematous,
an autoimmune disorder,
in which the body's immune system attacks its own healthy organs,
she rejected her doctor's suggestions for more aggressive treatment

as well as his warnings that she might die
if she stopped her cortisone,
and she returned to her native village in the Philippines.

Within three weeks she was back in the United States,
off cortisone and completely symptom-free,
with liver and renal function back to normal,
according to the doctor who treated her and
who published the facts about her case
in JAMA some four years later -
by which time she had also had a normal
pregnancy and delivered a healthy child.

To what did she attribute her miracle cure?
A healer in the Philippines had removed a curse placed on her!

The result of a primitive culture, you may say.
Perhaps.
But the mind/body principle extends to every culture!

**What's in your mind and heart is often quite literally,
or "anatomically",
what is in your body!** [11]

Obviously, then, we should strive for wholeness of mind and heart
that we might be physically whole.
We strive to free up our emotions and thoughts in order to
facilitate God's Blessing coming to us.

This means setting those who have wronged us totally free;
it means refusing to harbour any malice towards them
NO MATTER WHAT!
<u>FOR OUR OWN BENEFIT!</u>

A wise counselor states:
"Until you learn to heal the wounds of your
past you will never be whole!"
But so many people don't even know they're bleeding!
One of the things about forgiveness that is so hard is
we don't even know how to forgive ourselves,
or to ask for the forgiveness that we need.

Forgiveness is not something that you do for "them",
but what you do for yourself.
It means giving up the grudge because,
when you give up the grudge,
when you give up the blame,
you can give more love to yourself and to others.

Why do we hold onto unforgiveness?
There's a part of us - the deceptive intelligence -
that wants to hear the apology;
we want to see the punishment and the revenge.
We want to see the other person suffering.
We don't understand that that energy we're holding onto means
the less we can give and receive.
Unforgiveness literally blocks us!

Nelson Mandela was 46 years old when he
was sentenced to life imprisonment
on Robben Island in June 13, 1964.
His crime was opposing the apartheid regime
of his country, South Africa.
When asked about his positive attitude he replied:
"No one is born hating another person
because of the colour of his skin,
or his background, or his religion.
People must learn to hate.

If they can learn to hate they can be taught to love,
for love comes more naturally to the human heart than its opposite."
When he was finally set free from prison he
admitted he was tempted to hate
those who had incarcerated him, but he said
that to do so would give them the power
to imprison him for the rest of his life.
Mandela insisted: **Forgiveness set me totally free!**

Jesus was quite explicit in this regard in The Lord's Prayer:
**" 'Forgive us our sins, just as we have
forgiven those who have sinned against us.' "** [12]

This means that forgiving others holds
the key to our own forgiveness
and, indeed, our ability to receive the
full Blessing God has for us.

A pastor recalls how he had been involved in a
harsh struggle within his church and,
after sharing the incident with a friend,
received this dramatic response.
The friend stated categorically:
**"You must totally forgive them.
Until you totally forgive them you will be in chains.
Release them and you will be released."**

The pastor's response, after some consideration, was this:
"The ultimate proof of total forgiveness is
when we sincerely petition the Father
to let those who have hurt us off the hook.
I had to come face to face with this at one of
one of the fiercest times in my church.
I prayed for those who had wronged me to be forgiven.

I felt nothing; I just said it.

But then, after a few moments, it was as if the Lord said to me:
'Do you know what you are asking me to do?'
I thought that I knew and so I said, 'Yes.'

"The Lord then seemed to reply,
'Are you now asking Me to set them free
as if they had done nothing?'
That sobered me and I needed more time to think about it.
But while I was pondering that,
it seemed that the Lord reminded me of
what He had forgiven ME of.

I was frightened at the thought that He might reveal
some things for which He had forgiven me.
I then humbly prayed:
'Yes, Lord, I ask you to forgive them.'

"The Lord then seemed to say,
'Do you therefore mean that I should bless them and prosper them?'
Once more I needed some more time.
Then the Lord seemed to say,
**'What if I forgive and bless YOU in proportion to
how you want me to forgive and bless THEM?'**

"By this time," the pastor said, "I had no choice.
God had boxed me into a corner and I surrendered.
This time I sincerely and truly prayed for
them to be forgiven and blessed
as though they had done no offence."

The pastor confessed:
"It was the hardest thing that I had ever been asked to do,
but it was also the greatest thing I had been asked to do.

An unexpected blessing emerged as I began to forgive:
a peace came into my heart that I hadn't felt in years....

I made a decision for inner peace, but I found
out that I had to carry out that decision
by a **daily** commitment to forgive those who hurt me,
and to forgive them totally."

Unfortunately, this attitude runs counter to
our cultural attitudes which state:
"Revenge is mine, I will repay".
We feel that leaving God to settle the score is too slow a process;
we want resolution and 'vengeance' now!
We have been nurtured on such popular slogans as these:
"Don't get mad, get even!"
"Revenge is a dish best tasted cold"
"Treat them with contempt - distance yourself from them."
"Give them a cold shoulder - teach them a
lesson - they must be punished."

We become conditioned to deal with our
hurt feelings by suppressing them,
nursing our grudges in sulky silence,
refining our outward masks to hide our anger and bitterness.
But at what a personal cost!

A story is told about a snake that terrorized the children of a village
whenever they went out to play.
The elders of the village went out to talk to the snake
and asked it to please stop biting the children.
The snake agreed, and for the next few
weeks everything went well.
The children enjoyed playing outdoors and
returned home each day happy and safe.

The elders went to thank the snake,
but they discovered it battered, bruised and tied in knots.
When they asked the snake what had happened, the snake replied:
"Well, you told me to stop biting the children."
"That's right," they said, "we did tell you to stop biting,
but we didn't say to stop hissing."

It's important for us to express our feelings,
including the unpleasant ones,
because once they are "out" they lose their power over us;
they can't tie us up in knots anymore.

We can never escape the effects of what we allow to live
in our hearts and minds - the motivational center of our lives.

Just like the corroding shells of mustard gas used
in World War I, in the Battle of the Somme,
lying buried underground, now leak their deadly
poison into the earth and, years later,
their poison emerges to the surface and
kills farmers working their soil.

Father John Powell says,
"When you repress or suppress those things
that you don't want to live with,
you don't really solve the problem, because
you don't bury the problem dead -
you bury the problem alive and active inside you!"

Repressed emotions of unforgiveness block empowering faith!
Without forgiveness the power of faith does not operate
and God will not inhabit our "false" praise.

A pastor tells of working with a woman who
sought a more rewarding Christian faith.

He finally said to her:
"I think there's something that's keeping you spiritually stuck."
After exploring some possibilities, he suggested,
"Could it be unforgiveness?"

She phoned the pastor the next morning, after a
sleepless night, and again sought his help.
The pastor said, "We hadn't been talking long before her
bitterness towards her mother began spilling out.
I asked her to list on a sheet of paper all the injuries and
accusations she associated with her mother."
The next morning she came clutching a sheaf of papers.
She had been weeping.
"This is it," she said quietly, "This controls my life."

She handed the pastor five sheets of paper,
covered on each side with tiny script.
Entry after entry laid out a bitter indictment against her mother.
It added up to a life-long chronicle of personal loss.
They talked for an hour and, after much weeping,
she was able to repent of her unforgiving
spirit and release her mother.
Her face softened as if the clock had been turned back twenty years.

The pastor said, "Now you are ready to
receive something new from God."
She agreed and began a slow process of
reconciliation with her mother.
She said, "It feels like my soul is breathing again!"

Forgiveness breathes new life into our souls!

I watched a counselor being interviewed on television
A viewer posted this question on Facebook for the counselor:

"How do you forgive a family member that
you have constant contact with and,
though you forgive, the offence continues to happen?"

He replied, "You cannot forgive what you don't understand.
Understand what makes them do what they do.
It doesn't excuse them,
but it is so much easier to cope with a family member
when you understand they are broken in some way.
So, I cannot expect a radio that is broken to
play like a radio that's not broken.

Once you understand that you adjust your
expectations to deliverables
on the level of the person's capacity."

Everybody doesn't have the same capacity.
When you expect someone to love on a 'gallon'
level and they are a 'pint-person',
you're going to be frustrated the rest of your life.

The interviewer responded, "If you know you're a 'gallon person'
and you're dealing with a lot of 'pint-people' in your life,
should you let those people go; should you keep forgiving them,
keep forgiving, and forgiving the offence?"

The counselor replied, "First of all, adjust your
expectations to the level of their ability.
You can't have a life full of 'pint-people' if you're a 'gallon person'.
You're not even going to understand each other!
You might say, 'I need more from you.'
And they say, 'I'm giving you everything I've got.'
They are not lying to you!

They really are giving you all that they have
because they are 'pint people',
and they've emptied themselves out and
you have a capacity for more.

Irrigate your life with other relationships
that are not so dysfunctional -
'gallon people' ".

One of my favourite modern "gallon" Christians is Corrie ten
Boom, the Dutch Christian who was sentenced with the rest
of her family by the Nazis for the crime of hiding Jews.
She and her sister Betsie were sentenced to
Ravensbruck Concentration Camp
where they endured the harshest of treatments.
It was there that Betsie died.

Corrie ten Boom called herself a "Tramp for
the Lord" as she travelled the world
sharing her incredible witness for Christ.
As she reflected on her release from Ravensbruck,
Corrie was reminded of Betsie's prophecy
that they would both be out of the camp by New Year's Day, 1945.
Betsie had already died in the camp and been "released".

Thinking of the "what ifs",
Corrie recalled her sister saying:

**"There are no 'ifs' in God's Kingdom.
His timing is perfect.
His will is our hiding place.**

**Lord Jesus, keep me in your will.
Don't let me go mad by poking outside it."**

Corrie travelled all over Holland, other parts
of Europe and the United States.
But the place where the hunger was greatest was Germany.
Germany was a land in ruins, cities of ash and rubble,
but more terrifying still, minds and hearts of ash.
Just to cross the border was to feel the great
weight that hung over that land.

She then recalls this dramatic experience
where the passion of God's
forgiving power took possession of her life.

She tells how it was in a church in Munich that I
saw the former S.S. man who had stood guard
at the shower room door in the processing center at Ravensbruck.
He was the first of their actual jailers that
she had seen since that time.
And suddenly it was all there - the roomful of
mocking men, the heaps of clothing,
Betsie's pain-blanched face.

The man came up to her as the church was
emptying, beaming and bowing.
'How grateful I am for your message,' he said,
'To think that, as you say, Christ has washed my sins away.'

Corrie tells "His hand was thrust out to shake mine.
And I who had preached so often to people of the need to forgive,
kept my hand at my side.
Even as the angry, vengeful thoughts boiled
through me, I saw the sin of them.
Jesus Christ had died for this man; was I going to ask for more?"

She prayed, "Lord Jesus, forgive me and help me to forgive him."
She tried to smile, and struggled to raise her hand.

But she could not.
She felt nothing, not the slightest spark of warmth or charity.
And so she breathed a silent prayer.
"Jesus, I cannot forgive him. Give me your forgiveness."

Corrie then writes,
"As I took his hand the most incredible thing happened.
From my shoulder along my arm and through my
hand a current seemed to pass from me to him,
while into my heart sprang a love for this
stranger that almost overwhelmed me?"

So she discovered that it is not on our forgiveness,
or on our goodness that this world's healing hinges,
but on His.
When He tells us to love our enemies,
He gives, along with the command, the love itself.

And the result?
A Life of Passionate power!

Out of the brutality of her experiences during the war,
Corrie brings such a depth of spirit and
passion to this area of forgiveness.

She calls all people to receive God's forgiveness
and to realize the power of "forgetfulness".
She states this awesome Biblical truth that
when God forgives, He forgets!
He casts our sins into the deepest sea and
then puts up a sign with the words:
"No fishing!"

The tragedy for so many Christians is that, while
stating they are claiming forgiveness,
they refuse to develop this art of forgetfulness and instead
reach for their scuba gear!

Martin Luther, the great Protestant Reformer,
told of a dream he had one night in which the devil came to him
with a sheet of paper on which were written
a long list of Luther's sins.
The devil asked, "Is it true that you have done these things?"
"Yes," replied Luther, "but write across
that list in red ink these words:
'Jesus, His Son, cleanses us from all unrighteousness!' "

That's the key which fulfills our passion for power!

ENDNOTES

Preface
1. Mark 12:37 NKJV
2. Matthew 7:29 NKJV
3. Romans 1:14 NKJV
4. Romans 1:16 NKJV

Intro: "Where is the Love?"
1. azlyrics.com/lyrics/blackeyedpeas/whereisthelove.html

Ch. 1 – The Power of Passion
1. Ephesians 3:20 NKJV
2. goodreads.com/qyotes/21110
3. goodreads.com/quotes/34482
4. Peace, Love & Healing, P. 47, Arrow Books Ltd., London 1991
5. Psalm 26:2 NKJV
6. Job 23:10 NKJV
7. unpublished sermon
8. Luke 12:49 NKJV
9. Luke 3:16 NKJV
10. ccel.org/ccel/Wesley/journal/
11. pascalianawakenings.blogspot.ca/2007/11
12. II Corinthians 5:17 TLB
13. therevchrisyaw.blogspot.ca/2009/07
14. ligonier.org/learn/devotionals/john-calvin
15. Luke 3:16 NKJV
16. Romans 12:2 NKJV
17. Roman 12:2 TLB

Ch. 2 – The Power to Persist
1. en.wikipedia.org/w/index.
   php?title=Scent_of_a_Woman_(1992_film)&oldid=642642403
2. htb.org.uk
3. Daniel 3:17-18 NKJV
4. Daniel 3:25 NKJV

[5] Job 13:15 NKJV

[6] Romans 8:28 NKJV

[7] Luke 5:4 NKJV

[8] Luke 5: 5-6 NKJV

[9] Luke 22: 42-43 NKJV

[10] unknown source

[11] unknown source

[12] quoted in N.V.Peale STAY ALIVE ALL YOUR LIFE, books.google.ca

[13] artofmanliness.com/2009/04/25

[14] Hebrews 13:5 NKJV

[15] Matthew 28:20 NKJV

[16] Rocky V (1990 film) written by Sylvester Stallone

[17] goodreads.com/author/quotes/90212.Maxwell_Maltz

[18] Philippians 3:12-14 NKJV

[19] goodreads.com/author/quotes/18540.T_S_Eliot

[20] all-creatures.org/poetry/dontquit.html

Ch. 3 – The Passion to Overcome

[1] poemhunter.com/poem/invictus/

[2] Ephesians 6:10 TLB

[3] Galatians 2:20 NKJV

[4] Romans 8:31 NKJV

[5] poetryfoundation.org/poem/174659

[6] nytimes.com/books/first/h/higgins-daughter.html

[7] Philippians 4:13 NKJV

[8] Philippians 4:19 NKJV

[9] Philippians 4:6-7 NKJV

[10] cavaliersonly.com/poetry_by_christians_poets_of_the_past/poetry_by_
annie_johnson_flint/the red sea place

[11] Romans 5:2-5 NKJV

[12] I Thessalonians 5:18 NKJV

[13] Jeremiah 29:11 TLB

[14] II Corinthians 3:5-6 NKJV

[15] Psalm 55:22 NKJV

[16] I Peter 5:5-7 NKJV

[17] Ephesians 3:16-21 NKJV

[18] Colossians 2:6-7 TLB

[19] Romans 8:37 NKJV

Ch 4 – The Passion to Persevere

1. Shoes of the Fisherman (1963) Morris West
2. Hebrews 12:1-2 NKJV
3. Philippians 3:12-14 NKJV
4. Mark 5:28 TLB
5. John 11:21 NKJV
6. John 11:39 NKJV
7. John 11:40 NKJV
8. angelfire.com/on2/motivation/Peck.html
9. II Corinthians 5:7 NKJV
10. I Corinthians 2:9 NKJV
11. Colossians 1:11-14 TLB
12. goodreads.com/quotes/460515-thus-it-can-be-seen-that-mental-health
13. I John 4:4 NKJV
14. Romans 8:31 NKJV
15. Ephesians 6:10 TLB
16. II Corinthians 12:9 NKJV
17. II Corinthians 12:9-10 TLB

Ch. 5 – The Power of Passionate Prayer

1. I John 4:7-8,16 NKJV
2. John 15:4-5,7 NKJV
3. II Corinthians 9:8 NKJV
4. Philippians 1:6 NKJV
5. Philippians 4:19 NKJV
6. Luke 11:7 NKJV
7. Psalm 121:4 TLB
8. Luke 11:9 NKJV
9. Luke 11:13 NKJV
10. Luke 18:3 NKJV
11. Luke 18:4-5 TLB
11a. hourofpower.org/global/read_devotions_detail.php?tid=read&contentid=3457
12. Philippians 4:6-7 TLB
13. Psalm 46:10 NKJV
14. Romans 8:31-39 NKJV
15. I John 1:7 NKJV
16. I John 3:1 NKJV
17. James 5:16 NKJV

18   I Thessalonians 5:17 NKJV
19   Hebrews 13:5-6 NKJV
20   Psalm 37:4 NKJV
21   Romans 3:4 NKJV
22   Exodus 16:14-15 NKJV
23   Numbers 13:31, 33 NKJV
24   Numbers 14:8-9 TLB
25   Numbers 13:30 TLB
26   Romans 8:28 NKJV
27   Mark 11:22-24 NKJV
28   I John 5:14-15 NKJV
29   Romans 4:17 NKJV

Ch. 6 – Passion for the Possible
a   stuff.co.nz/world/europe/3261564/Seven-year-old-raises-NZ-220k-for-Haiti
1   Mark 10:27 NKJV
2   John 16:33 NKJV
3   Acts 2:26 Message Bible
4   I Samuel 30:6 NKJV
5   Jeremiah 29:11 TLB
6   I John 4:4 NKJV
7   II Corinthians 5:17 NKJV
8   Joshua 1:5, 7-9 NKJV
9   II Timothy 1:7 NKJV
10   I Peter 5:5-7 NKJV
11   Deuteronomy 31:8 NKJV
12   Deuteronomy 8:2-3 NKJV
13   Philippians 4:13 NKJV
14   Philippians 1:6 NKJV

Ch. 7 – Passion Through Praise
1   I Thessalonians 5:16-18 NKJV
2   I Thessalonians 5:18 TLB
3   Lamentations 3:17-20 TLB
4   Lamentations 3:21-26 TLB
5   Acts 16:23-24 TLB
6   Acts 16:25 NKJV
7   John 16:9 TLB
8   II Chronicles 20:12 NKJV

[9]   II Chronicles 20:15 NKJV
[10] II Chronicles 20:17 NKJV
[11] II Chronicles 20:21 TLB
[12] Ii Chronicles 20:22-23 NKJV
[13] I Corinthians 10:10 TLB
[14] Isaiah 55:8-9,11 NKJV
[15] Matthew 12:34 NKJV
[16] Proverbs 4:23 NKJV
[17] Matthew 12:34-35 NKJV
[18] Proverbs 18:21 NKJV
[19] I John 4:7-8, 12-13, 16 NKJV

Ch.8 – Passion for Purpose

[1]   Mark 8:35 NKJ
[2]   shmoop.com/hollow-men/poem-text.html
[3]   Matthew 10:30 NKJV
[4]   Jeremiah 1:5 TLB
[5]   Matthew 6:33 NKJV
[6]   patheos.com/blogs/yimcatholic/20111/02/because-of-the-note-sewn
[7]   II Corinthians 8:9 TLB
[8]   II Corinthians 12:9 NKJV
[9]   II Corinthians 12:9-10 TLB
[10] Isaiah 40:31 NKJV
[11] Zechariah 4:6 NKJV
[12] Proverbs 18:21 NKJV
[13] Numbers 23:8,20 NKJV
[14] Jeremiah 1:5 NKJV
[15] Psalm 109:28 NKJV
[16] Matthew 28:20 NKJV
[17] Exodus 14:13 NKJV
[18] Job 1:8 TLB
[19] Job 13:15 NKJV
[20] Philippians 1:6 NKJV
[21] I John 3:22
[22] II Corinthians 5:7 NKJV
[23] Romans 4:17 NKJV
[24] Romans 4:19-21 NKJV

Ch.9 – The Passion for Patience

1   II Chronicles 16:9 NKJV

2   James 1:2-8 NKJV

3   Romans 3:4 NKJV

4   Romans 12:2 NKJV

5   Ephesians 4:27 NKJV

6   Ephesians 6:13-14 NKJV

7   Hebrews 10:35-36 NKJV

8   Philippians 4:13 NKJV

9   I John 4:4 NKJV

10   Romans 8:31 NKJV

11   Exodus 14:13-14 NKJV

12   Luke 17:14 NKJV

13   Luke 17:14 NKJV

14   Ephesians 6:10-13 NKJV

15   Psalm 30:2 NKJV

Ch.10 – The Passion for Power

1   I John 4:10 NKJV

2   Galatians 2:20 TLB

3   I John 4:17 NKJV

4   II Corinthians 3:18 NKJV

5   Matthew 14:28-29 NKJV

6   Romans 8:32 NKJV

7   Galatians 5:6 NKJV

8   I John 3:1 NKJV

9   Ephesians 3:16-21 TLB

10   John 15:12 NKJV

11   Peace, Love & Healing, p17,21 Arrow Books Ltd. London 1991

12   Matthew 6:12 TLB